• Bartholom

WALK SUR

by Richard Hallewell
Illustrations by Rebecca Johnstone

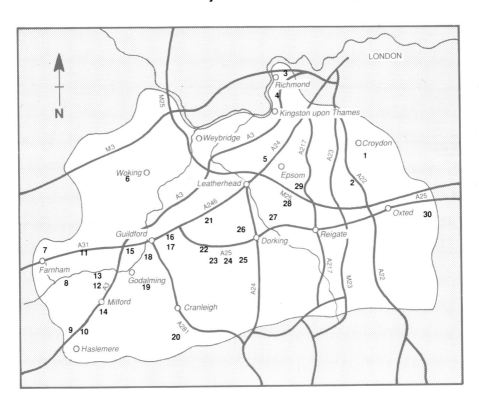

Bartholomew

A Division of HarperCollins*Publishers*

Published by Bartholomew, a Division of HarperCollins*Publishers*,
12 Duncan Street, Edinburgh EH9 1TA.

A catalogue record for this book is
available from the British Library.

First published 1992
© Bartholomew 1992

Printed in Great Britain by Bartholomew,
HarperCollins*Manufacturing*, Edinburgh.
Typesetting by John McKinlay, 11 King Street, Perth.

ISBN 0-7028-1807-0

About this book

This is a selection of walks in the county of Surrey, each of which can easily be completed within a day. The routes follow Rights of Way and accepted footpaths, and visit many of the finest beauty spots in the county, including the North Downs, the banks of the Thames and the many splendid heaths and areas of woodland which are scattered across the area.

Each route is graded according to its level of difficulty, and wherever specialist walking equipment is required this is specified on the contents page. There is a description of each route, including information on the character and condition of the paths, and a brief description of the major points of interest along the way, plus a detailed sketch map of the route to aid navigation. This guide supplies all the necessary information to complete each walk, but for some of the walks, where the route is particularly complicated, the additional use of a detailed map of the wider area is advised (see individual walks).

Car parks, where available, are indicated on the route maps, and the availability of public conveniences and public transport on particular routes is listed on the contents page and at the start of each walk. The location of all the routes is shown on the area map, at the front of the book, and at the beginning of the write-up of each walk there is a brief description of how the start of the route can be reached by car from the largest nearby town. Please note that a road map or atlas is essential if you wish to find your way around Surrey's complicated network of back roads.

The following introduction provides a summary of the geography, history, literature and wildlife of the area, plus a section of advice to walkers which you should read before setting out.

The serene and civilised landscape of Surrey has a great deal to offer the walker, and I hope that this selection of some of the many possible routes through this pleasant county will prove a useful guide.

Key

•••• Route	Marshland	**1 foot = 0.3m**
Metalled Road	Coniferous Woodland	**1 mile = 1.6km**
Bdwy Bridleway (Right of Way)	Broad-leaved Woodland	
50m Contour: shaded area is above height indicated	Railway	
	Ⓟ Parking	

Surrey

(Figures in italics refer to individual walks)

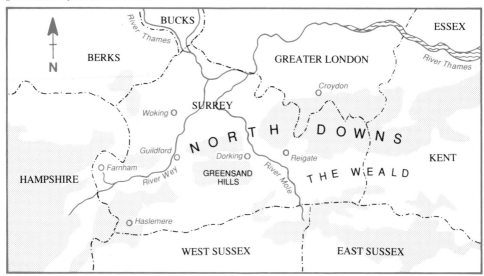

Many miles of excellent footpaths and bridleways criss-cross the quiet, leafy county of Surrey, providing a welcome contrast to the noise and bustle of the great city of London to the north. There is much to be seen when crossing the areas of heathery common land or strolling through the county's wide acres of woodland – some of the finest in the country. The low, steep ridges of the North Downs and the Greensand Hills provide miles of excellent, dry walking (since water doesn't lie on the chalky soils) and splendid views towards the South Downs of Sussex.

Although Surrey is a populous county, it is still perfectly possible to find routes away from the crowds – though never so far that there isn't a decent inn handy, often along the line of the route.

Surrey is not a large county of course – no more than 420,000 acres: 4 miles (64km) from Farnham in the west to Limpsfield in the east, and 30 miles (48km) north to south, from the River Thames to the Sussex border – but within its borders there is considerable variety, both in the geological shape of the land and in the uses to which, over the centuries, it has been put. This has created a patchwork of distinctive landscapes, and as the geographical grouping of the routes in this book might suggest, some of these landscapes lend

themselves to walking better than others.

The county is not as large as it used to be, having lost its administration over built-up areas such as Wandsworth and Lambeth, Richmond *(3, 4)*, Kingston upon Thames *(4)*, Wimbledon, Croydon and others at various stages since the Local Government Act of 1888. Since these areas formed part of the historic county of Surrey, walks through some of them are included in this guide, although they are all now part of Greater London.

The capital marches with Surrey for most of the county's northern border, although there are short borders with Buckinghamshire and Berkshire to the north-west. To the west the county marches with Hampshire, and to the south with West and East Sussex, while the county of Kent lies to the east.

The River Thames *(4)* flows through the north-western corner of Surrey but, that apart, there are only two rivers of any note in the county: the River Wey *(18)*, which flows north through Godalming and Guildford (where it passes through the line of the North Downs) to join the Thames at Weybridge, and the River Mole, which also flows northwards (passing through a more dramatic gap in the North Downs, north of Dorking) to join the Thames opposite Hampton Court. This dearth of rivers is caused partly by the light rainfall in the county, and

i

partly by the porous rocks which cover a large part of its surface. The ability of these rocks to absorb water has left a large number of dry valleys in the hill areas – around Box Hill *(27)*, for example – and even a river the size of the Mole is capable of disappearing beneath the round in dry weather; vanishing down swallow holes in the bed of the stream, then re-emerging further down the valley.

Geologically, Surrey is constructed of soft, young, sedimentary rocks composed of a mixture of rock fragments and the remains of living organisms which collected at the bottom of the lakes and seas which covered this area at various stages in the distant past. The oldest of the rocks is a form of clay, which was subsequently overlaid by greensand (a type of sandstone) and chalk. In the geological upheavals of subsequent eras, these layers of stone were raised up to form a crown above the area of the Surrey-Sussex border, and in turn this crown was gradually eroded by wind and water, revealing different layers of stone in different parts of the county: clay in the Weald straddling the Surrey-Sussex border) and ridges of the porous greensand and chalk in the Greensand Hills and North Downs respectively. Both of these ridges have similar physical characteristics, with long, gentle slopes to the north, and short, steep rises to the south, where the stone has been gradually eaten away.

None of the hills in Surrey are particularly high, but Box Hill *(27)* in the North Downs reaches 590ft (180m), while Gibbet Hill *(10)*, near Haslemere, is 895ft (273km) high, and Leith Hill *(25)*, in the Greensand Hills, is 965ft (94km), making it the highest point in the south of England. Compared to the peaks in the more mountainous, corners of the country, these heights are not great. The hills, however, are correspondingly easier to climb, and the low, flat nature of the surrounding countryside provides splendid views – enhanced in the case of Leith Hill by the construction of a stone tower on the summit in the 18th century, taking the total height of the hill above 1000ft.

The northern part of the county, beyond the North Downs, is composed of the various sands and gravels which have accumulated around the valley of the Thames, but since it has largely been built over by the southern extensions of the city of London, it is of comparatively little interest to the walker. This inexorable spread of the city has had a considerable effect on northern Surrey, transforming a number of old towns into boroughs of the capital, and creating a wider belt of suburban dormitories beyond the city itself.

For the rest of the county, the south-eastern corner, with its mass of small fields and woods, is not ideal walking country, so the majority of the routes are to be found in a central rectangle formed by the towns of Farnham, Haslemere, Reigate and Epsom, broadly corresponding to the areas of greensand and chalk, and including both major ridges of hills.

The area within this rectangle contains most of the finest scenery in Surrey: the wooded hills, approached by the characteristic sunken lanes which generations of rainfall and traffic have worn into the soft rock; the open downs; the pleasant farmland; and the rough moors and commons of heather, bracken, birch and pine which are such a feature of the area

It also contains the finest of the towns and villages, including smaller settlements such as Churt, Puttenham *(11)*, Peaslake *(23)* or (the most charming of all, perhaps) Shere *(22)*, and the larger towns of Farnham *(7)*, Guildford *(15,16,17,18)*, Godalming and Dorking.

The extensive woodland of the county is one of its most attractive features. Before man began systematically to denude the landscape, woodland was the typical ground cover of the majority of England, yet while many of the English counties have lost virtually all of their substantial forests, Surrey has retained (or regained) considerable tracts of wooded land.

The major reason for this is that successive generations have found the county's soils to be less than ideal for the pursuit of intensive agriculture. They are thin, stoney and fast draining on the chalk hills, damp and clinging in the clays of the weald, and simply infertile in the bleak moors and commons of the north-west.

Nevertheless, early attempts were made to cultivate Surrey and, by the mid 14th century, the woods and heaths had been pushed back to the extent that the best of the land in the county was under cultivation of one sort or another. In the 1340s, however, the Black Death caused great reductions in the local population, and in the wake of this disaster much of the land reverted to its former state. In some areas – most notably in the rough heathland of the north-west – it remained in that condition until the 19th century; cultivated only at subsistence level, if at all.

The nature of the old Surrey heathland can still be seen in small remaining patches of heather, bracken and birch which are scattered around the western end of the county: Frensham *(8)* or Puttenham Common *(11)*, for example, or Ockley Common *(12)*, dotted with peat holes and criss-crossed by meandering streams and dry, sandy tracks.

The history of the woodland areas is more complicated since, by the late medieval period, landowners were already seeing the value of timber production, and a certain amount of replanting had already begun; both of coppice woods (ie of hazel, alder, etc, which would be cut back every few years to provide wood for such purposes as fencing, firewood and charcoal, and of plantations of larger trees such as beech and oak for the construction of buildings and boats.

A further increase in replanting began in the late 17th century, inspired in part by the ideas of John Evelyn *(see Literature)*, and there was a further burst of activity in the 19th century; largely with the objective of improving the landscape. Surrey's present woodland is therefore the result of centuries of conscious commercial and landscape planning, which has produced something rather different from the tangled, untamed forest which once covered the county.

The first visitors to this primeval 'Surrey' of wild beasts and unbroken broad-leaved woodland would have been the people of the early Stone Age – the Palaeolithic period – whose crude stone implements have been found in some numbers in the county. The presence of these artefacts is hardly surprising, since the chalk soil of the North owns is a rich source of flint, and continued to be an attraction to the more advanced peoples of the middle Stone Age – the Mesolithic period – who

arrived in southern England between 10,000 and 4000 BC. There is greater evidence of Mesolithic occupation in Surrey than in any other district of South-East England.

Neolithic remains (ie, those from around 3000 BC onwards: the period which produced monuments such as Stonehenge, in Wiltshire) are less plentiful, which would seem to suggest that these early agriculturalists found less to please them in the dense Surrey woods than had their hunter/ gatherer predecessors, whose dependence for food on the fruits of the forest, fish, and wild birds and animals, obviated the need for them to clear more than a living space for themselves in the woods, or to try to till the difficult soils.

One feature of the Surrey landscape which probably dates back to this period is its oldest road: the Pilgrims' Way *(15,16,17,22)*. The exact route of the Way is impossible to establish, but from earliest times there appears to have been a well-used track linking Winchester, in Hampshire, with Canterbury, in Kent: a distance of around 130 miles (210km). In Surrey, this track followed the line of the North Downs, through Farnham and Guildford, then on along the ridge of hills, north of Dorking, Reigate and Oxted. The value of the ridge was that it was easily followed, while the chalk soil ensured dry walking – as it does to this day.

The continued importance of Winchester and Canterbury throughout the Roman and Saxon periods ensured that the route remained in common use, and the traffic it carried was further boosted by the growing fashion for pilgrimages during the late Saxon and early medieval periods. Initially, the prime attraction was St Swithin, a much loved Bishop of Winchester (d. 862), and tutor to both King Ethelwulf of the West Saxons and his youngest son Alfred (later Alfred the Great). His shrine was popular for some centuries following his death, but from the late 12th century onwards the attraction of Canterbury proved the greater. In 1170 Thomas à Becket, the Archbishop of Canterbury who had opposed the will of King Henry II, was murdered in Canterbury Cathedral. By 1173 he had been canonised, and a cult swiftly developed, with stories being spread of miracles performed before his tomb. Chaucer's *Canterbury*

Tales tells of a pilgrimage from Southwark, in London, but similar pilgrims from the South-West would have followed the old Neolithic route by the North Downs.

Bronze and Iron Age relics are comparatively rare in Surrey, but there are a few of the characteristic hill-top forts of the Iron Age period in the county; notably on the peak of Holmbury Hill *(24)* and at Anstiebury, near Coldharbour *(25)* (both in the Greensand Hills). The people of southern England, at this time, were of Celtic stock, and Surrey appears to have been divided between two tribes, called by the Romans the Regni and the Antribates, who had their capitals at Chichester and Silchester respectively.

The Romans had first arrived in Britain in two expeditionary forces, under Julius Ceasar, in 55 and 54 BC. No permanent settlement was made at that time, but the Romans increased their knowledge of the island, and subsequently there was regular trade and communication between the Roman province of Gaul and the tribes of southern 'England'.

About a century after these first approaches, the Emperor Claudius sent an army under Aulus Plautus to annexe the southern part of Britain: partly in response to the rise of an anti-Roman faction in the British tribes, and partly in order to open his reign with an auspicious military victory. This was duly achieved, and though the Romans were subsequently to have difficulties with the tribes of the west and the north, and with the rising of Boudica and the Iceni in East Anglia in AD 60, the conquest of the South-East was swift, decisive and, following the Battle of the Medway, without serious opposition.

All but the northern part of Surrey continued to be something of a backwater during the three and a half centuries of Roman occupation, and though the remains of towns, forts and large numbers of villas have been found in neighbouring counties such as Kent and Sussex, the density of population in Surrey appears to have remained comparatively low. Very few notable remains have been discovered in the county, though archaeologists have unearthed a villa in the pleasant woodland of Ashtead Common *(5)*, near Epsom.

The most important and far reaching event in the Roman occupation (as far as Surrey was concerned) was the creation of a new capital at Londinium, on the Thames. From early times it must have provided a significant market for agricultural produce, while the roads built between the capital and the south coast provided access to the heart of the county. The two main roads were Stane Street (running through Ewell – and past Ashtead – to Chichester) and the road between London and Lewes (on the Sussex coast).

The Roman occupation of England came to an end in AD 407, brought about by a mixture of attacks by the tribes of northern Britain and the continent and the general collapse of the Roman Empire into warring factions. The net result of this withdrawal was to leave the Celts of Romanised southern Britain without any adequate defence against the increasingly numerous attacks.

Soon after the Roman withdrawal the Germanic invaders from the continent began to establish their first permanent settlements, and by AD 450 the Jutes had founded a kingdom in Kent. Over the following century, the majority of what is now termed 'England' was colonised by the Angles and the Saxons, while the Celts were driven from the more prosperous land, and confined to areas such as Cornwall, Wales and the North-West.

By the end of the 6th century, the conquerors had divided the area into a number of kingdoms: Northumbria in the far north, Mercia (between Wales and the Wash), East Anglia, Kent and Wessex. The Saxon sub-kingdom of Surrey was caught at the junction of Kent, Mercia and Wessex, and seems to have changed hands between its more powerful neighbours during the centuries of intermittent power struggles which followed the Germanic conquests. Certainly it appears to have been a part of Offa's Mercian kingdom in the late 8th century, before reverting to the control of Wessex during the early part of the 9th century, during which time King Egbert was establishing himself as virtual overlord of the greater part of England. Subsequently, a number of kings of Wessex were crowned at Kingston-upon-Thames *(4)*.

During the period of Saxon rule the southern parts of Surrey remained sparsely populated, but large expanses of the forest which covered the county were gradually felled; at first to allow living space for the herdsmen who brought their cattle to graze in the forest during the summer months, but later to clear ground for permanent agricultural settlements. There were still no major towns to the south of the North Downs, but Guildford *(15,16,17,18)*, by an important crossing point on the River Wey, seems to have originated in this period. The town is first mentioned in the will of the most successful of the kings of Wessex, Alfred the Great, who died in 900.

Alfred is principally remembered for his resistance to the incursions of the Danes, who began a series of invasions of England in the early 9th century. They succeeded in conquering Northumbria and East Anglia by the 870s, before turning their attentions to Wessex. Initially, Alfred had little success against the Danish army, but in 878 he defeated it at Edington, and was able to force the invaders back into the north and east of England – the area which became known as the Danelaw. The Danes were granted control of this area in return for their agreement to adopt Christianity.

The Danelaw extended no further south than Essex, so under the terms of the agreement Surrey remained under Saxon control.

The kings of Wessex gradually regained control of those parts of England granted to the Danes, and (with the exception of a break between 1016-1042 when the throne was held by King Canute, of the Danes, and subsequently by his sons) retained their hold on the country until the Battle of Hastings in 1066.

The period following William the Conqueror's victory over King Harold saw the introduction of feudalism into England, and the growth of the power of both the Crown and the Church. It is ironic, therefore, that the most famous historical landmark in Surrey, Runnymede, is emblematic not of the strength of the Norman kings, but of the restrictions which could be placed upon them.

King John (1167-1216) is traditionally remembered as the wicked younger brother of Richard the Lionheart and, as such, is a staple element of the Robin Hood stories. He was probably not as bad a monarch as his reputation would suggest, but he was certainly an outstandingly devious one, and his intrigue and treachery left him an isolated figure within his own realm. In 1207 the Pope appointed Stephen Langton Archbishop of Canterbury. This was much against the wishes of John, who was keen to bring the English church more under the control of the Crown, but, following his excommunication by the Pope in 1212, he finally succumbed to the pressure and accepted the appointment. Despite this belated acceptance, the English barons remained at odds with John over the arbitrary nature of his rule at home and a string of defeats which England had suffered on the continent at the hands of the French. In 1215, under the leadership of Langton, they forced him to sign the Magna Carta at Runnymede (by the Thames, in the North-West of the county).

It is by no means certain that John intended to abide by the agreement he had signed, but by 1216 he was dead, and the charter – essentially a definition of the privileges of the major magnates in the realm – came, in time, to be seen as one of the cornerstones of English liberty.

There are few buildings in Surrey from the Norman era, but the thick walls of the keeps at Guildford and Farnham *(7)* both date back to the 12th century, while the ruins of Waverley Abbey, by the River Wey near Farnham, belong to the 13th century.

Waverley was the most important of the 12 religious houses established in Surrey during the period of the Church's growth in power. It was founded in 1128 by 13 monks from Normandy, on land granted by the Bishop of Winchester, and is of particular importance because it was the first Cistercian house established in England. Very little now remains of the once extensive buildings of the abbey, which suffered (as did all such structures) from a mixture of vandalism and neglect following the Dissolution of the Monastries in the 1530s, during the reign of Henry VIII.

As a result of these losses, the finest remaining ecclesiastical buildings in Surrey are the parish churches. Some of these date back to Norman times – St Martha's *(17)*, for example, on the ridge of the North Downs to the east of Guildford – but there are fine examples covering every period up to the Victorian era, The county's only cathedral, Guildford, is of an even more recent vintage, having been built in our own century.

The building, which occupies a commanding position on Stag Hill, to the north-west of the city, was designed by Sir Edward Maufe. Construction began in 1936, but due to the intervention of the Second World War it was 1961 before the cathedral was completed and consecrated.

Guildford was only the third new Anglican cathedral to be built in England since the Reformation; a fact which demonstrates the decline in wealth and power of the Church which followed Henry VIII's break with Rome. Initially, the Crown was the primary beneficiary; assuming the position of head of the Church of England, and selling off whatever forfeited land and buildings it had no use for to the highest bidder. As a result, Henry was able to strengthen central power and fill the coffers of his treasury. One result of this new found wealth was the building of palaces: the outward show of the stature of any ruler.

Henry began building in 1530, and by the end of his reign he owned over 50 houses, the most important of which were Hampton Court (on the north bank of the Thames, just upstream from Kingston-upon-Thames), and the Palace of Nonsuch, near Epsom. This latter was started in 1538, and was the most imposing of all his buildings: a huge structure built around two courtyards, with the southern facade flanked by two vast octagonal towers. The building was, sadly, demolished in 1687, having been left incomplete on Henry's death 1547 and subsequently sold off to a private owner during the reign of his daughter, Queen Mary – evidence of the short time which it took for the Crown to lose the wealth which it had accumulated.

Mary's successor, Elizabeth I (her half-sister), inherited a bankrupt treasury. This rather limited her scope for extravagant gestures, but it was not in her nature to be a palace-builder in any case; her parsimony was legendary, and with the example of the swift rise and fall of her predecessors' finances to encourage her, she sought alternative ways of impressing her subjects – or rather of allowing them to impress her.

The Tudor monarchs had drawn the teeth of the great barons of the realm to the extent that Elizabeth need hardly fear a repeat of the treatment meted out to King John. The feudal system was dead, and the powerful men no longer owed their position in the realm to the number of armed men at their disposal, but rather to their position at court, and to the sinecures and monopolies which they could garner from the queen or her ministers. Those who were successful, or who aspired to success, began to build country seats for themselves – no longer castles, but elegant country houses – in the hope that, in one of her annual royal progresses through the southern counties, the Queen might deign to accept their hospitality. The cost of entertaining the accompanying entourage was potentially ruinous, but the lure of possible advancement was such that there was never any shortage of willing hosts.

A number of these Elizabethan mansions were built in Surrey – Sir William More's Loseley House *(15)*, in the farmland to the west of Guildford, is a fine example – but, for the most part, Surrey remained a poor and somewhat unfashionable area, and despite a steady, if slow, improvement in the agriculture of the area, the most profitable occupations of the period were the small-scale rural industries: most importantly the production of iron, glass *(20)* and cloth.

Surrey did not begin to become fashionable as a place to live until the end of the 17th century, but from then up to the present day there has been a continuous process of urbanisation (or suburbanisation) in the county. The process started with the increasing fashion for country houses which developed amongst the gentlemen of the realm in the Restoration period. This led to the building of a number of fine mansions in Surrey (particularly in those areas now covered by west and south London). Around the same time, John Evelyn, with his passion for garden design and tree-planting, was starting the process of moulding the county's landscape into an idealised bucolic form.

Those parts of Surrey further from the capital remained largely untouched by this slow revolution, principally because the roads – scarcely improved since Roman times – were in such an appalling condition that they represented an obstacle to travel rather than an aid. In particular, the clay soils of the Weald could become practically impassable in wet weather.

This problem was not tackled until the advent of the turnpikes linking London and the south coast in the mid 18th century. These roads were built for the use of the stage-coaches, and thus had a firm, smooth surface, but the number of good, passable roads in Surrey remained small until well into the 19th century, and large areas of the county remained much as they had been for centuries. As soon as the turnpikes were built, however, the villas and mansions followed them, and developers and builders soon realised that there was a ready market for houses in this previously neglected area.

The main reason for this new interest in rural living was a simple desire to escape from the increasingly crowded and filthy capital. In addition, however, there was a growing idealisation of the countryside in general amongst the expanding urban population.

On a popular level, this resulted in the growing use of the counties around London for holidays and recreational purposes. In Surrey, this movement started with the development of the North Downs (and later spa towns such as Epsom) as health resorts, and eventually led to such curiosities as the rise of hill walking as a popular hobby (Surrey – and the North Downs in particular – was one of the first areas where hill walking was practised by significant numbers of people). On a more elevated level, this idealisation led to the perception of Surrey as one vast landscape garden, and also to the creation of a large number of splendid individual gardens within the county; the most important of which are the famous Royal Botanic Gardens at Kew (4) (in London, by the River Thames: now outside the county boundaries).

Other important gardens include the Royal Horticultural Society's garden at Wisley (east of Woking), which was started by G F Wilson in 1878, and the Winkworth Arboretum (19) near Godalming, but there are many more. One of the chief attractions of Surrey to gardeners was its

poor, sandy, acidic soil (particularly in the west of the county), which proved to be ideal both for arboreta and for the propagation of rhododendrons and azaleas: exotic flowering shrubs originally found in the similarly poor soils of the Himalayas.

One of the landscape gardeners who greatly influenced the development of the gardens at Wisley was Gertrude Jekyll (1843-1932), who was brought up in Bramley, near Godalming, and became a leading figure in what has been called the 'Surrey school' of gardening. The main characteristic of this movement was a retreat from formal borders and planting to a more natural arrangement of herbaceous borders and wild gardens. This studied recreation of the 'natural' through art was echoed in the work of her closest collaborator: the architect Sir Edwin Lutyens (1869-1944).

Lutyens was brought up in Thursley (between Milford and Hindhead), and was to become the dominant architect of his generation, being chosen to design such major government works as the Viceroy's Palace in Delhi. However, he is more fondly remembered for his large output of small country houses and villas (many in Surrey). In style he followed the lead of architects of the previous generation such as Norman Shaw (who also produced a large number of buildings in the county), who in turn had borrowed heavily from the vernacular styles of the English regions. In Surrey this involved the use of red brick, half-timbering, hanging tiles and tall chimneys. Surrey is fortunate in that a large number of the original, vernacular houses of this type still exist, along with the buildings of Shaw, Lutyens and others which were influenced by them.

Ironically, this interest in 'natural' gardens and Surrey's vernacular architecture coincided with the swift erosion of the old way of life in the county. The building spree put the cost of land, houses and rents beyond the means of most locals, and the new villas were purchased by émigrés from the London smog. In the early 19th century, the incomers would generally stay only for the summer, but after the railway system began to expand into the area in the 1830s, it became increasingly easy for people to commute to London from the country: an arrangement which continues to suit many of Surrey's residents today.

The railways had a major impact on Surrey, but that other staple of the Industrial Revolution, the canals, made less of an impression. As early as 1651 Sir Richard Weston was authorised to make the River Wey navigable from Weybridge (at the junction with the Thames to Guildford), and in 1760 the additional four miles (6.5km) of the Godalming Navigation *(18)* were added. In 1815 the Wey & Arun Canal *(20)* was opened, forming a direct link between London and Portsmouth, but it was never a commercial success and closed in 1871. Likewise, the Basingstoke Canal *(6)* – a western spur of the Wey Navigation opened in 1794 – was closed by 1910, never having been profitable.

Industrial relics are not the essential stuff of Surrey, however. The county as it is today has been produced by a blend of two separate influences: the labours of the many generations of largely anonymous farmers who, from the Stone Age onwards, slowly cleared the forest and laid out the fields in their attempts to grind a hard living from the poor soils, and the tradition of the improvers and incomers, who built houses and remoulded the landscape to fit their own ideals and tastes. There is little doubt which tradition has triumphed, for good or ill, in the majority of the county; but though the suburban sprawl has overwhelmed some areas, others retain the serene beauty which first encouraged the incomers to settle here, and it is still possible to turn off the main roads, follow one of the narrow, sunken lanes into the wooded hills, and start walking along ancient ridge tracks which have been significant highways through the land since the first tribesmen reached this part of England.

Literature

If Surrey's historical associations are somewhat scant, its literary connections are more formidable; principally during the county's fashionable heyday in the 19th century, but starting as early as the 17th.

In 1620, the great diarist **John Evelyn** was born at Wotton House, about three miles (5km) west of Dorking on the A25. Although his royalist sympathies drove home out of England in 1649, and his work and many interests subsequently kept him in London for much of the time, he had a considerable impact on the family estate (which he inherited from his elder brother in 1699). This was principally through his interest in landscape gardening, which was to find an outlet both at Wotton and the nearby Albury Park.

Perhaps Evelyn's greatest impact was on the woodlands of the area. Timber was in great demand at that time – not least to supply the needs of the Navy – and the Royal Society (of which Evelyn was one of the first Fellows) asked him to look into the problem. The result was *Sylvia: or a Discourse on Forest Trees*, published in 1664: a practical guide to arboriculture which sparked off a wave of planting. Evelyn himself is thought to have been responsible for much of the early planting on Leith Hill *(25)*.

Not far to the north of Wotton is the estate of Polesden Lacey *(26)*. The current house (owned by the National Trust, and open to the public) was built in the 19th century, but the previous house on the site was bought in 1796 by the playwright and politician **Richard Brinsley Sheridan** (author of *The Rivals, School for Scandal*, etc), along with the neighbouring Yew Tree Farm. Sheridan had just married for the second time, and was still optimistic about his political career; he was living well beyond his means, however, and by the time of his death (1815) he was quite penniless.

Few of Surrey's literary figures were actually born in the county, but the writer and political radical **William Cobbett** (1762-1835) was an exception. He was born at his father's inn in Farnham *(7)* (then the 'Jolly Farmer'; now the 'William Cobbett', in Bridge Square) and died within a few miles of the town. In the course of a full life, however, he travelled extensively, spending some years abroad in both France and America.

Cobbett's output was immense and controversial, and covered a wide range of subjects, but he is probably best remembered for his political polemics, which made trouble for him on more than one occasion. In a less controversial vein, he was responsible for the first publication of *Parliamentary Debates* (now Hansard) and, near the end of his life, he published his famous series of sketches of the English countryside, *Rural Rides.* In this book he included descriptions of his home county, and unfavourable observations on the spread (even at that early date) of the genteel suburbia of London into the rustic world of his youth.

Thirty years after Cobbett's birth, in 1793, the novelist **Fanny Burney** was visiting in Surrey, and made the acquaintance of a colony of French emigres at Juniper Hall, near Box Hill *(27)*. The colony – which included such notable characters as Mme de Staël and Talleyrand – were refugees from the French Revolution, and amongst their number was General D'Arblay. Fanny and the general were married at Mickleham in 1794, but the impecunious couple were unable to set up a home of their own until 1797, when the money earned by her successful third novel, *Camilla,* allowed them to build Camilla Cottage in West Humble, by Box Hill.

The D'Arblays left for France in 1802, but Box Hill (above all other sites in Surrey) continued to have a fascination for writers. **Jane Austen** seems to have visited the hill on one of her visits to nearby Great Bookham, and used it as the setting for a scene in *Emma*, while **John Keats** also visited the site, while writing *Endymion*. The writer who is most closely associated with Box Hill, however, is the novelist and poet **George Meredith**, who moved to Flint Cottage in 1864 and remained there until his death in 1909. Meredith was a keen walker of the hills surrounding his home, and a great lover of the Surrey countryside, which provides a background for many of his novels, including his most popular work, *Diana of the Crossways* (1885).

The great Victorian poet, **Alfred Lord Tennyson,** also has a strong connection with Surrey, having moved to Haslemere in 1868, where he was to live until his death in 1897. In the following year, Charles Dodgson (**Lewis Carroll)** died in Guildford *(15,16,17,18),* while on one of his visits to the family home in Castle Hill. Some relics of Dodgson are kept in the local museum.

A further Victorian writer with Surrey connections was the novelist **George Eliot** (Mary Ann Evans: author of the novels *Middlemarch, The Mill on the Floss,* etc), who lived at Witley *(14),* south-west of Godalming, from 1877 until her death in 1880.

In the 20th century, the greatest figure associated with the county was the novelist **E M Forster,** who (though often travelling abroad) kept a house at Abinger Hammer – about five miles (8km) west of Dorking on the A25 – between 1902 and 1945. In addition, two popular classics were written in Surrey in the early years of the century: **J M Barrie's** *Peter Pan* (1904) at Farnham *(7),* and **Arthur Conan Doyle's** *The Hound of the Baskervilles* (1902), which he wrote at his house in Hindhead *(9, 10),* where he lived between 1896 and 1907.

Natural History

Though Surrey is a small county, it contains a wide variety of habitats within its borders. Furthermore, the complex geology of the area has created a landscape which dictates that these habitats exist in small intermingled patches rather than in large blocks; thus, at Box Hill, the slopes of the hill are of chalk, yet the top of the hill is overlaid with a layer of clay-with-flints, which supports a different range of flora and fauna. Thus, within a single walk a variety of habitats can be seen.

In general terms, the habitats can be divided into a number of broad groups – **Woodland, Forestry, Parkland, Freshwater, Farmland, Heathland and Downland.** The basic animal and plant types of these habitats are described below, and the numbers of those routes which feature each are listed after the headings. Naturally, given the complexity of the area, some routes are listed more than once.

Woodland *(all)*

The county's woodland is one of its great glories, and no route in this book fails to pass by or through a substantial plantation of some kind, while some routes pass through trees for the majority of their length *(1,5,9,10,14,19,20,23,24, 25,27)*. The nature of these woods varies from the scrub **birch, alder, hazel** and others which can be found in areas where trees have recently recolonised previously open ground *(14,28)*, to areas of mature, broad-leaved woodland including trees such as **oak, beech** and **ash,** often mingled with species of conifers such as **Scots pine, Corsican pine** and **larch** *(1,3,5,11,17,20,23,24,25, 27)*. In addition, there is one arboretum *(19)*, and some woods where the native evergreens – **holly, juniper, yew** and **box** – can be found in some profusion *(16,27)*.

Woodland mammals in the area include **badger, grey squirrel** (no red), **dormouse** and **roe deer.** Of these, the ubiquitous grey squirrel is likely to be seen regularly, while the shy roe deer may be surprised in quiet clearings. The badger and dormouse are both nocturnal and it will require great good fortune to see either.

Amongst the specifically woodland birds in the county are the **great spotted, lesser spotted** and **green woodpeckers** (this last is very common, and its strident 'laugh' can often be heard in the woods), plus the **nightingale, nuthatch, treecreeper, goldcrest** and **tawny owl** and **sparrowhawk,** plus a variety of **tits** and **finches.**

Forestry *(20,21,23,24,25)*

There is comparatively little commercial forestry in Surrey, but this book does include two routes which follow forest walks through such plantations *(20,21),* and dense stands of conifers can be found elsewhere. These plantations are of relatively little interest to the naturalist. They provide cover for **rabbit, fox** and **roe deer,** but the trees are generally close together, thus keeping sunlight from the forest floor and inhibiting the undergrowth necessary to sustain the smaller mammals and insects at the bottom of the food chain.

Such birds and animals as are present will be the same as for the **Woodland** list.

Parkland *(1,3,7,29)*

This grouping includes any area of open, low-level grassland which is not given over to agriculture. The wildlife present is a mixture of that listed for **Woodland** and **Farmland,** but one of the routes has a specific attraction for the naturalist. Both Farnham Park *(7)* and Richmond Park *(3)* originated as deer parks (ie, they were maintained for hunting purposes), and Richmond has the distinction of retaining large herds of both **red** and **fallow deer.** The deer are well used to the presence of people in this busy park, but walkers are requested not to approach them too closely as they are not necessarily as tame as they appear.

Freshwater *(4,6,8,18,19)*

Extensive areas of water are rare in Surrey (with the exception of the reservoirs in the north-west of the county), but there are some rivers *(18)*, canals *(6,18)* and small ponds *(3,8,19)* with routes running by them, plus the mighty River Thames *(4)* in the north of the county.

The principal attraction of these areas of freshwater is the large variety of bird life which they attract, including the **heron** and **great-crested** and **little grebes, cormorant, coot** and **moorhen,** plus **Canada goose, gulls** and **terns.** Ducks include **shelduck, mallard, teal, shoveler, tufted duck** and **goldeneye,** while **redshank, greenshank** and **curlew** are present, and, amongst the smaller birds, **pied** and **yellow wagtails** and the splendid **kingfisher.**

Farmland *(2,15,17,22,26)*

A considerable amount of Surrey is given over to farmland – either arable or pasture – but it tends not to coincide with the best walking areas, so few of the routes in this book encounter it for much of their distance.

Fields are sometimes fringed with hedges, which provide cover for **finches, sparrows, robin, linnet, wren, blackbird** and others. Larger birds to be seen in the fields include **carrion crow, magpie** and **lapwing,** plus **pheasant, partridge** and **quail,** and **redwing** and **fieldfare** in the winter months. Watch for **swallow, swift** and **martins** in the summer months.

Heathland *(8,10,12,13,28)*
The heaths are a great feature of Surrey, and range from the wet heath at Ockley *(12)* (including the Thursley Nature Reserve, notable for its large number of **dragonfly** species) to drier, sandy heaths such as those at Frensham *(8)* and Puttenham *(11).*

The cover is generally a mixture of **heathers, grasses** and **bracken,** with an admixture of **blaeberry** and other small shrubs. Where grazing animals are no longer present, the heaths are often punctuated with clumps of scrub woodland and **Scots pine,** which flourishes on the poor soil.

This type of habitat attracts birds such as the nocturnal **nightjar,** plus the **woodcock, snipe, jack snipe, little owl, yellowhammer, stonechat, whinchat** and **wheatear.** Watch also for **lizard, grass snake** (entirely harmless) and **slow worm.**

Downland *(2,16,27)*
The downs are areas of open grassland on low hilltops. At one time they would have been given over to grazing, but nowadays they are generally free of animals, which has led to the encroachment of scrub woodland in places. The main attraction of the downs lies not in their bird or animal life, but in the wide variety of plants which inhabit the chalk and clay-with-flints, including **sainfoin, milkwort, scabious, eyebright, speedwell** and a variety of **thymes** and **vetches.** During the summer months these high pastures are alive with butterflies and insects attracted by this wide range of flowers.

Advice to Walkers

The first thing to do is to make sure that you pick a route which is within the range of your capabilities. Check the grading system at the front of the book and make a realistic assessment of your abilities before looking for a walk within the suitable grade.

None of the walks included is particularly gruelling, but many of the paths in the area are covered with a loose, dry sand, which makes the routes more tiring than the lengths given might suggest. By the same token, the sand and chalk soils which cover much of the county tend to absorb surface water very quickly, so unless it has been raining recently there is little need to worry about surface water, and waterproof footwear is not an important consideration on most walks.

The routes in this book are generally clear, but navigation can be complicated on some of them. It is a curious fact that the more gentle and civilised a landscape is, the more problems arise with finding the route through it; largely because of the proliferation of paths and tracks in areas of high population. In addition, some of these routes – notably those in the Greensand Hills *(23,24,25)* –

pass through areas of dense woodland which are criss-crossed by numerous footpaths and bridleways, and finding the exact route can sometimes be difficult. Bearing these problems in mind, it is suggested for some routes (see individual walks) that a detailed map of the wider area be used in addition to the sketch map in the book. Failing that, no walk in Surrey is so quiet that someone will not be along soon to offer advice.

In the wooded areas, and on the open heaths, commons and downs, the adjoining paths – some of which are shown on the sketch maps – are generally open to the use of the public. When passing through farmland or areas of housing, however, take care to stick to the signposted rights of way, and not to stray onto private land.

The weather in Surrey is usually fairly clement, but check the weather forecast before setting out, and if in doubt take light waterproofs – better safe than sorry.

There are no wild animals in the area which are likely to prove dangerous, but you are advised to stay clear of farm animals if possible; they are not always as docile as they look.

1 Selsdon Wood

Length: 2 miles (3km)
Height climbed: 150ft (45m)
Grade: C
Public conveniences: Car park
Public transport: Numerous bus services to
Selsdon

*A route following some of the numerous paths
through this pleasant area of mixed woodland
and parkland. Paths good.*

Selsdon is a residential area of Greater London,
slightly to the south-east of Croydon. Although it
has largely been swallowed up in the general
sprawl, there are still extensive areas of open
ground and woodland surrounding the housing. An
example is Selsdon Wood, now in the care of the
National Trust.

To reach the wood, drive to the southern end of
the town on the A2022, then turn onto Old Farleigh
Road. When the housing ends to the left of the
road there is a car park.

There are a great many paths through the
woods and open parkland in this area, and
although a route is suggested below, a glance at
the map will suggest a number of potential
alternatives and extensions.

For the route shown, walk straight on beyond
the end of the car park, with a grassy bank climbing up to the right. Follow the path through two
bands of trees, and the open areas beyond each,

before entering a thicker plantation of mixed,
broad-leaved woodland and continuing with a high
fence to the left.

Just before the fence at the far end of the wood
is reached, a clear track heads off up the slope to
the right. Follow this up and over the hill, ignoring
the tracks to right and left, and continue until (near
the edge of the wood) a clear track cuts back hard
to the right.

Take this track and, after a short distance, there
is a choice of three paths. Take the middle one and
continue. At the next junction go left and continue
(ignoring paths to either side) past a fenced well
and on to an area of open ground. Follow the path
across this and into the woods on the far side. The
path continues clear (once again with tracks leaving
to either side) to a four-way junction. Take the
tarmacadam track directly ahead; leading out of the
woods to the top of a grassy slope, at the bottom of
which is the car park.

2 Farthing Downs

Length: 3-6 miles (5-9.5km)
Height climbed: Undulating
Grade: B
Public conveniences: Car park
Public transport: Occasional bus service to
Chaldon from Redhill

*A signposted circuit through farmland and
woodland, using some of the numerous paths
around this excellent viewpoint. Paths good.*

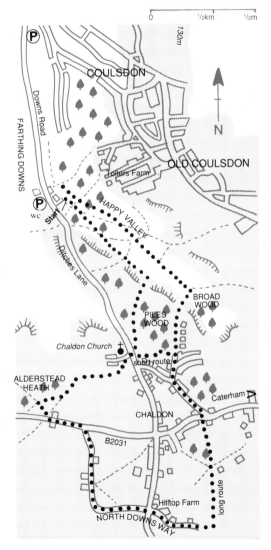

Farthing Downs is a low, open, chalk ridge rising
to the south of Coulsdon, with its northern end in
Greater London, and its southern in the open
country. The views from the ridge are splendid,
and there are a great many paths laid out both
across it and in the surrounding countryside.

To reach Farthing Downs, drive south into
Coulsdon on the A23, then turn left onto Marlpit
Lane (for Caterham) and take the second turn to the
right into Downs Road. Follow this road up onto
the ridge, ignoring the first, small car park, and
continuing to the large one at the far end of the
ridge. Beside the car park there are shops, plus a
large notice-board giving details of the footpaths
around the ridge.

Two specific walks have been laid out through
the farmland to the south; described on the notice-
board and signposted along the way. Both of the
routes start by dropping down the track which leads
off from the little pavilion containing the notice-
board; starting through fine mixed woodland and
then emerging into the open grassland of Happy
Valley.

Walk on along the top of the fields until the
route cuts to the right; through a band of trees and
over cultivated farmland (please stick to the path
here) to Chaldon Church. From this point there is a
choice: for the longer route, turn right past the
chuch and follow the path down to Alderstead
Heath and beyond *(see map)*. For the shorter route,
continue along the road towards Chaldon for a
short distance, then turn left on a clear path which
leads up past Piles Wood, then turns left to return
to the foot of Happy Valley. Turn left up the
central track along the valley floor to return to the
car park.

3 Richmond Park

Length: Up to 8 miles (13km) or more
Height climbed: Undulating
Grade: A/B/C
Public conveniences: At various car parks
Public transport: Numerous bus and underground
services throughout London

*A broad area of open parkland and woodland,
criss-crossed with numerous footpaths, tracks
and public roads. This historic park contains
two small lakes and a number of fine buildings.*

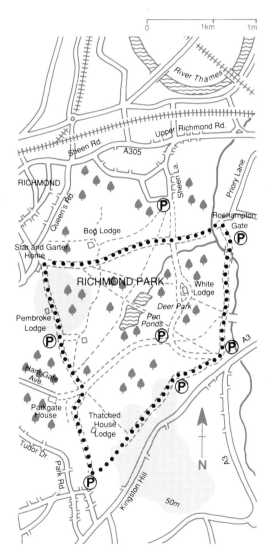

Richmond Park is a huge area of open, rolling
grassland punctuated by scattered areas of mature,
mixed woodland. It is situated in the south-west of
London, to the east of the old borough of
Richmond. This pleasant quarter of the city first
came to prominence as the site of the Plantagenet
kings' Sheen Palace, which was replaced by Henry
VII's new Richmond Palace around the start of the
16th century (nothing survives of this building now
but the gateway).

The land behind Richmond was used by
successive kings as a hunting ground and, in 1637,
Charles I enclosed a large part of the area for use as
a deer park, though he was forced to allow the local
people continued access to the pathways across the
park. Private shooting in Richmond Park was
stopped in 1904, but the deer remain: several
hundred red and fallow deer which roam freely
across the grassland. **Please note that walkers
should not approach these animals.**

The area which King Charles enclosed covers
over 2000 acres, and is now crossed by a large
number of metalled roads, bridleways and
footpaths, connecting seven car parks spread
throughout the park. The walk shown on the map,
around the edge of the park, covers about eight
miles (13km), but many alternative short cuts and
extensions will suggest themselves once you start
walking.

Amongst the features of the park are White
Lodge (built for George II in 1727, and now used
to house the Royal Ballet School) and the Pen
Ponds: two small lakes in the centre of the park.

Richmond Park opens at 7am and closes each
day at dusk.

4 Kew to Kingston

Length: 8 miles (13km)
Height climbed: Negligible
Grade: A/B/C
Public conveniences: Richmond; Kingston
Public transport: Numerous bus services throughout London

A lineal route following the bank of the River Thames through parkland, woodland and housing. Paths good and plenty of activity on the river.

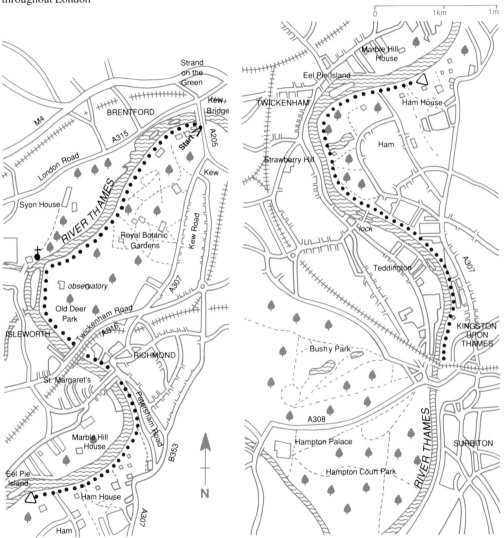

Walk 4

The River Thames rises near Cirencester, in the Cotswold Hills, and then flows around 210 miles (340km) to the North Sea; starting through tranquil countryside and then flowing through the heart of London. It is the largest, busiest and most important river in England.

This walk follows the southern bank of the Thames from Kew Bridge to Kingston-upon-Thames. The path is a good one, and follows the side of the river for the whole way, providing fine views of the busy river traffic, and of the towns and houses on either bank. The whole route need not be followed; it can be joined at a number of points along the river.

Starting from Kew, walk down to the river by the side of Kew Bridge and turn left along the clear track by the riverside (to the right it is possible to follow the river for about four miles (6.5km) to Hammersmith). On the far side of the river is the pleasant district of Strand on the Green while, almost immediately, the wooded park of the Royal Botanic Gardens starts over a wall to the left. The Gardens were founded in 1759 by the mother of George III. They were later enlarged, improved and given to the nation by Queen Victoria. In addition to the huge range of trees and plants, the Gardens have a number of plant houses and ornamental buildings as well as miles of tranquil pathways.

Shortly before the end of the Gardens – which continue by the river for over a mile (1.5km) – Syon House appears on the far side of the river. The house is basically Jacobean, but it was refaced in 1825, and has a splendid interior by Robert Adam (1761).

After the Botanic Gardens end, Old Deer Park starts to the left. In the middle of this there is an observatory built in 1729 to a design by William Chambers, who was also responsible for the ornamental buildings in the Botanic Gardens. On the far side of the river is the village of Ilseworth, with its 15th-century church tower clearly visible.

The river continues to swing round to the left, and at the end of Old Deer Park is the elegant town of Richmond, with its new water frontage designed by the architect Quinlan Terry.

Richmond originally came to prominence as the site of palaces of the Plantagenet and Tudor kings, but it reached its heyday in the Georgian period when it became the favourite retreat of both royalty and fashionable London society. Features of the town are nearby Richmond Park *(3)*, plus the elegant town green and the surrounding 18th-century architecture. The waterfront at Richmond is very popular at weekends and during holidays, and there are bars and restaurants by the riverside.

After leaving the town, the river swings round to the right and passes through a more rural area. On the far side of the river is Marble Hill House (1724), standing in parklands which run down to the water. The house was built by the architects Pembroke and Morris, and was given by George II to his mistress, Henrietta Howard. On the left-hand side of the river is Ham House: a splendid 17th-century mansion. Both these houses are open to the public (check with tourist offices for times).

The river now swings back to the left, with open ground on the near side and a built up area including Twickenham, Strawberry Hill and Teddington across the water. Beyond Teddington Lock (the highest tidal point on the River Thames), the river swings right again, passing sailing and rowing clubs as it follows the final two miles (3km) to Kingston-upon-Thames.

Kingston dates back to Saxon times, when a number of kings were crowned here, but nowadays it is a rather unexceptional suburb. To finish the walk here, climb up the steps by the side of the road bridge.

Beyond Kingston it is possible to follow the river for a further three miles (5km) along the north bank to Hampton Court, but the most interesting part of the river ends at Kingston.

5 Ashtead Common

Length: 3¹/₂ miles (5.5km)
Height climbed: Negligible
Grade: B
Public conveniences: None
Public transport: Numerous rail and bus services
to Ashtead

*A route using some of the numerous footpaths
and bridleways through this area of dense,
mixed woodland. Some navigation required;
paths generally good. Excellent views.*

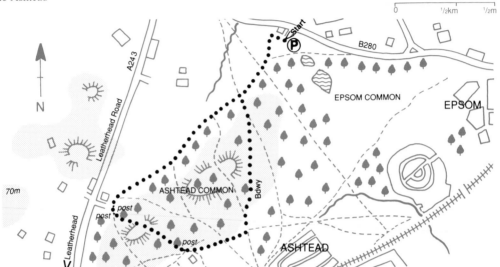

Ashtead Common is covered by a splendid carpet
of mature woodland, with some particularly fine
old oak trees scattered throughout the wood. There
are a number of footpaths and bridleways
throughout the area, some of which have been used
in the route below. Other possible routes will be
obvious from the map.

To reach the Common, drive west from Epsom
on the B280. The car park is to the left of the road,
about two miles (3km) from the centre of the town.

For this route, walk west from the car park (ie,
turn left if you are facing the road) to join a clear,
rough footpath running along the edge of the wood,
with fine views across farmland to the right.
Continue along this path, passing various
junctions, but always walking straight on along the
route signposted for the Leatherhead Road.

As the path approaches the road, a building

appears to the right. At this point, turn left onto a
fainter path marked by a white-topped post,
heading into the heart of the woods. When the path
splits, go to the left (once again marked with a
post) and climb up onto the brow of a low hill.
There has been considerable fire damage to the
woods here, but the trees are gradually reasserting
themselves.

Drop down the far side of the hill and continue
until you reach a post with a blue arrow on it, at
which point another path crosses the way. Turn left
onto this. When the path splits, keep to the right,
and follow a narrow path through dense scrub
woodland to a junction with a clear bridleway.

Turn left onto this and follow it through the
centre of the woods (passing the site of a Roman
villa) back to the original path on the far side of
the common. Turn right to return to the car park.

6 Brookwood

Length: 4¹/₂ miles (7km) via golf course
Height climbed: Negligible
Grade: B
Public conveniences: St Johns
Public transport: Numerous train and bus services
to Brookwood

*An attractive towpath running through
farmland, woodland and housing by the bank
of an old canal. Possible return across a golf
course and along the public roads.*

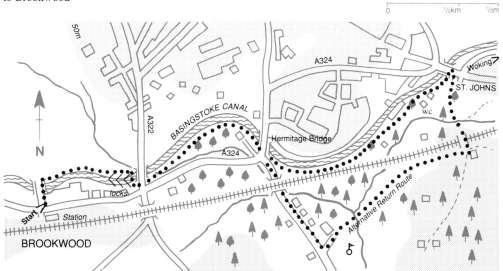

Brookwood is a small town on the western edge of
Woking – about three miles (5km) from the town
centre on the A324. Park in the centre of the town
and look for the lane which starts directly opposite
the entrance to the railway station. Walk down to
the foot of this and cross the bridge over the canal,
then turn right and join the towpath by the canal-
side. This is the Basingstoke Canal: completed in
1794 and running some 40 miles (60km) from the
Wey Navigation to Basingstoke.

Follow the towpath past two locks. Then, at
the third, cross over the canal on a footbridge and
continue along the far side: under a road-bridge
and on through an increasingly rural area of woods
and fields. Pass under a further road-bridge, then
continue to a third, at St Johns.

From this point, either return by the same route
or else (for a slightly longer return route) climb up
to the road and turn right, then immediately right
again. When this road swings round to the right,

carry straight on along a tarmacadam path, heading
across an area of open parkland, then into dense
woodland.

Follow this path across a railway line, then
turn right along a path running parallel to the line
with a fence to the right. Follow this until a rough,
raised path heads off to the left across the fairway
of a golf course. Follow this path straight across
the course (making sure that no one is playing as
you cross each hole) and into more woodland. At
the end of the path, turn left down a driveway to
join a public road.

Turn right along the road, keeping a careful
watch for traffic. It is necessary to cross to the far
side of the road when it passes under the railway
bridge (since the pavement is on that side), and
then to recross beyond. Cross with care, as this
road can be busy. When the road reaches a
junction by the Hermitage Bridge, drop back down
to the canal and return by the original route.

7 Farnham Park

Length: 3 miles (5km)
Height climbed: 160ft (50m)
Grade: C
Public conveniences: Farnham
Public transport: Numerous bus and rail services to Farnham

A series of clear tracks running through an area of open grassland and scattered woodland, and passing the semi-ruinous Farnham Castle.

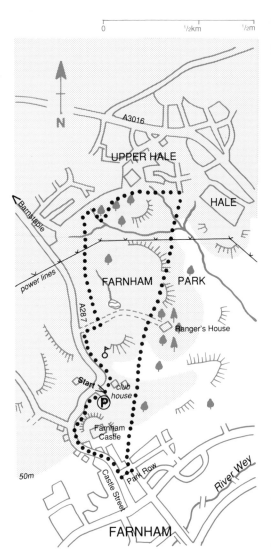

The beautiful country town of Farnham sits on the far western edge of Surrey and, in addition to some of the finest town architecture in the county, it contains the old castle of the Bishops of Winchester and the deer park which once belonged to it – now Farnham Park.

To reach the park, drive north from the centre of the town on the A287 road signposted for Barnstaple (Castle Street), and turn right, just beyond the edge of the town, into a large car park.

Walk back to the entrance of the car park, then turn right along a tarmac path running by the road, with a golf course to the right. Follow this for a short distance until a metalled road cuts right. Turn down this and follow it to the far edge of the golf course. At this point, leave the road and head left on a faint but visible footpath, leading off across the rolling grassland of the park towards some houses on the horizon.

Follow the path up to the edge of the houses, then turn right towards a fringe of woodland along the edge of the park. Skirt this until a tarmac path appears running through it, then follow this until it ends at a junction with another footpath. Turn right along this, back across the grassland and scattered woodland of the park. Continue down the slope to the edge of Farnham, noting the impressive walls of the castle to the right. Walk down the narrow lane at the end of the path, then turn right along Park Row to reach the splendid Castle Street, with its elegant Georgian architecture.

Turn right and follow the right-hand pavement up the hill, out of the town and back to the car park. Along the way, the road passes the entrance to the castle (open to the public throughout the year), the old keep of which dates back to the 12th century.

Walk 7

8 Frensham Country Park

Length: 4 miles (6.5km)
Height climbed: 90ft (30m)
Grade: B
Public conveniences: Car Park
Public transport: Regular bus services to
Frensham from Haslemere and Farnham

*A route using some of the many fine footpaths
and bridleways in this area; passing through
open heath and conifer and broad-leaved
woodland, in addition to passing two large
ponds. Paths good.*

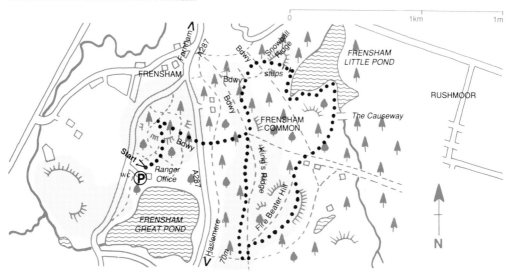

To reach this fine area of heath and woodland, turn
west (right if you are driving south) off the
Farnham to Haslemere road (A287), about three
miles (5km) south of Farnham town centre. The
Country Park is signposted at the junction.

Park in the large car park by the Great Pond
and head northwards (away from the pond) on one
of the numerous sandy tracks. Make for the point
where the main bridleway crosses the A287. Cross
the road and follow the straight track ahead, up
onto King's Ridge.

Once on the ridge turn left along a footpath
through pine trees; initially running parallel to a
larger bridleway. Follow this path through one
junction (marked by a seat), then downhill through
woods to join a bridleway. Cross this and go right
at the fork immediately afterwards. Follow the
path across a further bridleway and climb up to the
ridge beyond.

From the junction on the top of the ridge turn
right, down a flight of wooden steps, then continue
down the hill to join the path running round the
Little Pond. Turn right along this, to the end of a
narrow inlet, then turn left around the broad
promontory on the southern side of the pond until
the small feeder stream is reached and the wooden
causeway over it.

Ignore the causeway and carry straight on to a
four-way junction. Go straight across this and
continue; watching for two paths which should be
visible to the left. Cross over to these and follow
the furthest left: up onto the ridge of Fire Beater
Hill. At the far end of the ridge, this path joins a
bridleway. Turn left along this for a short distance
to a four-way junction. Turn right here, then
immediately right again along a clear footpath
through fine woodland, leading along King's
Ridge to rejoin the original route.

9 Devil's Punch Bowl

Length: 2¹/₂ miles (4km)
Height climbed: 350ft (100m)
Grade: B
Public conveniences: Car Park
Public transport: Regular bus services to
Hindhead from Haslemere and Farnham

*A series of marked paths and tracks through
an area of fine broad-leaved woodland, heath
and farmland. Paths generally clear. A
leaflet describing features along the route is
available at the car park.*

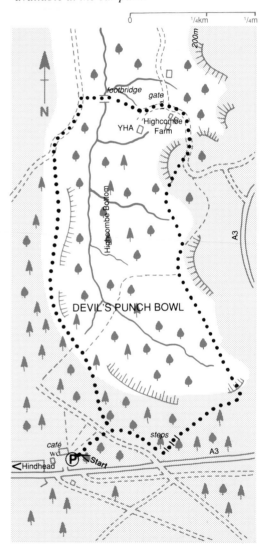

Hindhead is a small town about three miles (5km)
from Haslemere, at the junction of the A3 and the
A287 Haslemere to Farnham road. To reach the
start of the route, drive north from this junction
along the A3. After a short distance the edge of
the town is reached and a large car park appears to
the left.

Walk to the side of the car park furthest from
the road and look for the signpost for the 'Punch
Bowl Nature Trail'. From near this point there is a
fine view over the broad, deep, sandstone valley
(now owned by the National Trust).

Turn right along a clear track which runs
through dense woodland along the back of the car
park, and continue until a steep flight of steps leads
down to the left. From the foot of these, continue
along a clear track; skirting a marshy area to the
left. The track runs through open heath at first,
and then through mature woodland.

Turn left when the track joins a metalled road.
Continue past the entrance to Highcombe Farm,
following the sign for the Youth Hostel (YHA).
When the road splits again keep left (once again
following the YHA sign); through a gate and along
a clear track. Continue along this until it starts to
swing round to the left, in front of the small
redbrick hostel, at which point continue straight
ahead; following a well-worn track down into the
wooded valley bottom ahead, and then crossing a
wooden footbridge over a small stream.

Climb up the path directly opposite and then,
at the top of the bank, turn left along a clear track
which climbs gently, through mature conifer and
broad-leaved woodland, back to the start of the
walk.

Walk 9

10 Gibbet Hill

Length: 2 miles (3km)
Height climbed: Undulating
Grade: C
Public conveniences: Car Park
Public transport: Regular bus services to
Hindhead from Haslemere and Farnham

*A series of clear tracks and rough footpaths
through an area of conifer and broad-leaved
woodland and open heath. Fine views. A
leaflet describing some of the details along
this route is available from the car park.*

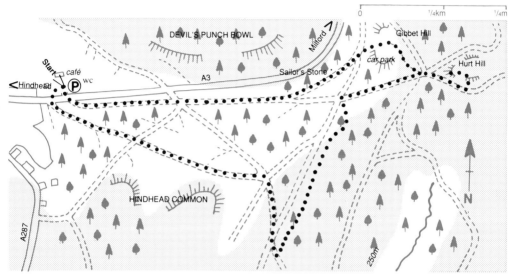

To find the start of this route, follow the directions given for *Walk 9*.

Walk to the entrance of the car park and cross the A3 (**Please take care here as this is an extremely busy road**). Directly opposite the entrance there is a sign for the Gibbet Hill Nature Trail (laid out by the National Trust and marked by white posts) at the start of a track.

Turn left along this track, which runs broadly parallel to the main road with dense woodland to the left and the open ground of Hindhead Common to the right. After a short distance there is a five way junction. Carry straight on, keeping an eye open for the Sailor's Stone to the left of the track. This commemorates the murder of a travelling sailor here in 1786.

A short distance beyond this a car park opens up to the right. Walk through this, and on to the heathery peak of Gibbet Hill (where the two

murderers of the sailor were hanged in chains) just beyond. There are fine views from this point.

From the brow of the hill, turn right down a narrow path; passing through broad-leaved woodland to reach a six-way junction. A short diversion (following the posts marked with two white dots) leads to another viewpoint on Hurt Hill; otherwise, turn right (track marked by white post) and follow the track to a five-way junction. This time take the path furthest to the left (the smallest of the alternatives) and follow it through dense woodland to join a clear track by another viewpoint and a seat. Double back to the right along the clear track; crossing a four-way junction and then continuing to a further five-way junction by a seat.

Swing left (staying on the main track) and continue, across Hindhead Common, back to the A3.

Walk 10

11 Puttenham Common

Length: 1-3 miles (1.5-5km)
Height climbed: Undulating
Grade: B/C
Public conveniences: None
Public transport: Regular bus service to
Puttenham from Guildford

*Three marked routes through fine mixed
woodland and across open heath of heather
and grass. Paths good.*

The pleasant little village of Puttenham sits in the
shadow of the ridge of the Hog's Back; just off the
A31, four miles (6.5km) to the west of Guildford.
To reach to start of the walk, drive south from the
village on the unnumbered road for Elstead. Ignore
the first car park to the right of the road and
continue to the second one: about two miles (3km)
from the village, just before the road passes The
Tarn *(see map)*.

Puttenham Common is an area of mixed
woodland and open heathland; in places covered by
thick scrub of pine and oak woodland, in others by
ling heather or grasses. Parts of the common are
now designated sites of special scientific interest
for their wildlife, while the string of ponds at the
western edge of the common provides a habitat for
a wide variety of waterfowl.

Three walks have been laid out through this
pleasant area; all starting from this car park: the
white, green and red routes – one, two and three
miles (1.5; 3 and 5km) respectively. These walks
are marked by posts of the relevant colour and are
easily followed.

The longest route (the red route) takes in the
greatest variety of landscape, but it is worth
making a diversion at the start of the walk to
follow the green route down to the edge of The
Tarn before doubling back to join the others *(see
map)*. The red route then continues through the
woodland and grassland up the western edge of the
common, before cutting right along a section of the
North Downs Way, then turning right again and
returning through the heart of the common. The
going under foot is generally dry, but the paths are
of loose sand, which can make walking tiring.

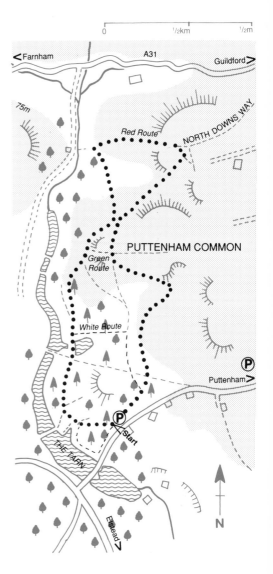

Walk 11

12 Ockley Common

Length: 2¹/₂ miles (4km)
Height climbed: Negligible
Grade: C
Public conveniences: None
Public transport: Regular bus services from Godalming to Elstead

A level route following some of the many footpaths and bridleways of this area; passing through open heath and broad-leaved woodland. Includes Thursley National Nature Reserve. Paths good.

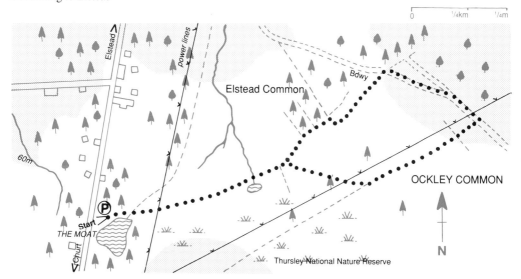

The village of Elstead is two miles (3km) west of Milford on the B3001. To reach the start of this route, turn south from Elstead on the unnumbered road for Churt. A mile and a half (2.5km) from the centre of the village turn left at the signs for 'The Moat', and park in the small car park in the pine trees by the side of a large pond.

Start walking away from the road, with the pond to the right. At first the clear path runs through the pines, but it soon emerges onto sandy heather moorland; crossing a small stream and passing the turn into the duck-boards and paths of Thursley National Nature Reserve. This is an area of valley bog, particularly notable for the range of species of dragonflies which it supports.

Carry straight on towards the trees ahead. Ignore the first two tracks which come in from the left (one at the edge of the trees, the next a little

further on) and continue until the path reaches a four-way junction. Turn right and follow a clear track along the edge of the woods, with the heath to the right.

After a short way there is a junction, and a bridleway heads off to the left. Ignore this and continue along the main track, which now starts to swing round to the right in an area of fine birch woodland. Continue along this until it reaches a line of pylons, carrying power lines through the wood. At this point turn right along the path which follows the line of the pylons. Almost immediately there is a four-way junction. Go straight across this and continue, out onto the heath again.

This clear track follows the line of the wires at first, then swings right to rejoin the original track. Turn left to return to the start of the route.

13 Elstead

Length: 5 miles (8km)
Height climbed: 100ft (30m)
Grade: B
Public conveniences: None
Public transport: Regular bus services to Elstead from Godalming

A pleasant route along paths, tracks and public roads, passing through heath and mixed woodland (and crossing a golf course) and providing fine views from an open hill. Navigation tricky in places.

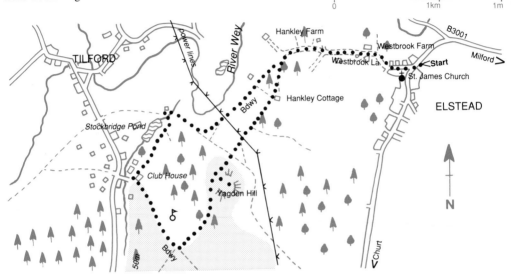

Elstead is a small, pleasant village, two miles (3km) west of Milford on the B3001. For this route, turn south from the centre of the village onto the minor road for Churt. Park near St James Church and turn right, just before it, on Westbrook Lane.

Follow this road until the tarmac ends and the track beyond splits. Take the right-hand track and follow it through woodland (ignoring two paths cutting off to the right) to a three-way split (with the entrance to Hankley Farm to the right). Take the track furthest to the left and follow it through the wood to the corner of a field where it splits again.

Follow the right-hand track across a four-way junction and out of the woods onto an area of heath. The track passes under some power lines, just beyond which there is a further split. Follow the right-hand track; gently climbing up Yagden Hill, the top of which is visible ahead.

Follow the track over the right shoulder of the hill (a short detour leads up to the top) and down the other side on a sandy track, which soon joins a golf course to the right. Carry straight on down to the bottom of the slope, where a bridleway crosses the track. Turn right on this, across the golf course (ignoring tracks to the right and left) and on down to the club house.

Turn right through the car park and carry on, with a fairway to the right and a wood to the left. At the end of the course there is a pond to the left, at the far end of which the track splits. Go left, down to a T-junction, then right along a clear track.

After crossing a stream there is a split. Go left (following the bridleway arrows) then carry straight on, along a ridge above the valley of the River Wey, back to the junction at the entrance to Hankley Farm.

14 Witley Common

Length: 1, 2 and 2 miles (1.5, 3 and 3km)
Height climbed: Negligible
Grade: C
Public conveniences: Information Centre
Public transport: Regular bus services to Milford from Guildford and Haslemere

Three gentle, signposted walks through a picturesque and extensive area of mixed woodland. A leaflet is available from the information centre at the start of the walks, explaining some of the features along the routes.

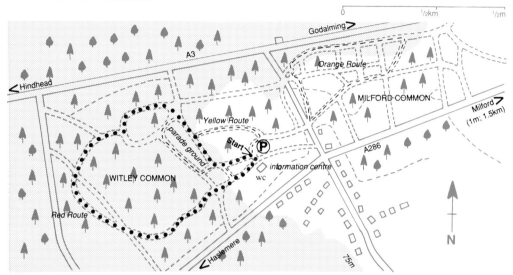

Witley Common and adjoining Milford Common are areas of mixed woodlands and open heath, maintained by the National Trust and open to the public. To reach them, drive a mile (1.5km) south of Milford on the A286 road for Haslemere, and turn right onto a minor road signposted for 'Witley Centre'. Turn first left to enter the car park. Please note that this car park closes at 6pm, and is only open from April to October.

There are three routes in total: two starting from the car park – the Yellow Route (one mile/ 1.5km) and the Red Route (two miles/3km) – and the third from the far side of the road, opposite the

entrance to the car park – the Orange Route (two miles/3km). All three are clearly marked, and a booklet available at the Information Centre gives details of what can be seen on each.

Witley Common was at one time part of the estate of Witley Manor, and belonged to the Kings and Queens of England, but it was sold off in the time of Elizabeth I. In more recent years both Witley and Milford Commons were used as army camps for British and Canadian troops during the Second World War; indeed, the large flat area in the centre of Witley Common is still known as the parade ground.

15 Loseley House

Length: 5 miles (8km)
Height climbed: 200ft (60m)
Grade: B
Public conveniences: Guildford
Public transport: Numerous train and bus services to Guildford

A pleasant walk along a series of footpaths, bridleways and public roads through open farmland and the mixed woodland along the North Downs. Paths good and the route passes a splendid old stately home.

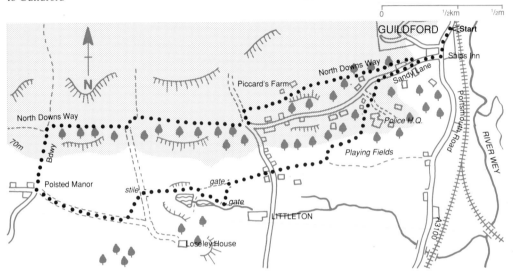

Loseley House is a fine Elizabethan mansion (built in the 1560s for Sir William More) in the pleasant farmland to the south-west of Guildford.

For this route, park in Guildford and walk south on Portsmouth Rd (A3100). Continue until the Ships Inn appears to the left, and Sandy Lane cuts off to the right. Turn up this road and follow the pavement to the left. When the road swings to the right, carry straight on along a public footpath, and when this reaches a metalled road, go straight across and continue along the footpath which starts directly opposite through an area of police housing.

Continue along this path, with playing fields down to the left and a wooded bank to the right. When a junction is reached, turn right and follow a clear path past fields down to a public road. Go straight across this and continue beyond, across one field and then into a second. After entering the second field, turn left, down to a track, then

right. At the next junction turn right, then swing left, noting the fine views of Loseley House over a large pond to the left.

Follow the path as it crosses an unmade road, then swings left to join the main road into Loseley Park. Turn right along this to the junction at Polsted Manor, then turn right again and follow a bridleway uphill through a narrow wooded cut. At the brow of the hill turn right at the junction with the North Downs Way, and follow it through the fine woodland along the top of the ridge. At the first junction turn left, then right almost immediately. At the second, turn left for about 150yds, then right again at the sign for the North Downs Way.

Continue along a clear track through pleasant farmland until Sandy Lane is reached once again, then turn left to return to Portsmouth Road.

Walk 15

16 Merrow

Length: 5 miles (8km)
Height climbed: Undulating
Grade: B
Public conveniences: Car Park
Public transport: Regular bus services from
Guildford

*A series of clear footpaths and bridleways
through an area of mixed woodland and open
grassland on the ridge of the North Downs.
Excellent views.*

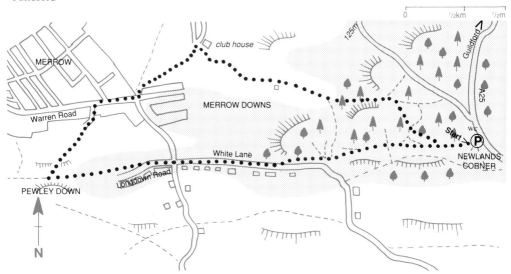

The residential district of Merrow sits on the
eastern edge of Guildford, just to the north of an
area of woodland and open grassland known as the
Merrow Downs: an area which contains a great
many fine footpaths and bridleways.

To reach the start of this route, drive east from
the town centre on the A25. Two miles (3km)
beyond the edge of the town the large Newlands
Corner car park appears to the right of the road.
Park in the car park (noting the fine southerly
views), then walk straight through it and on along
the clear bridleway which continues beyond,
through a fine mixed wood. Ignore the numerous
paths leading off to either side and continue until
the track joins with a public road (White Lane).
Continue along this until it reaches a four-way
junction, then carry straight on along Longdown
Road. When this swings to the left, carry straight
on along a clear track leading to the open hill of
Pewley Down, which provides further fine views to
the south.

A short way onto the Down there is a gap in the
hedge to the right. Turn through this and follow
the rough path beyond downhill to join a concrete
driveway which then climbs up into an area of
housing. Turn right along Warren Road and, when
this swings round to the right, go half-left onto the
open grassland of Merrow Downs.

There are a variety of vague paths across this
area: simply head towards the golf club house on
the far side of the Downs and, once there, look for
the clear track which leads away from the club
house. Follow this track across the golf course and
into the woods; past a small cottage and on along an
open ride, noting the fine yew trees by the track-
side.

Continue (ignoring the paths to either side)
until the traffic on the A25 becomes clearly
audible, then look for a fork in the path and head
right, back to the car park.

17 Chantries

Length: 6 miles (9.5km)
Height climbed: 450ft (140m)
Grade: A
Public conveniences: Guildford
Public transport: Numerous rail and bus services to Guildford

A picturesque route along a sequence of bridleways, footpaths and public roads; passing through woodland and farmland and providing very fine views. Navigation tricky in places.

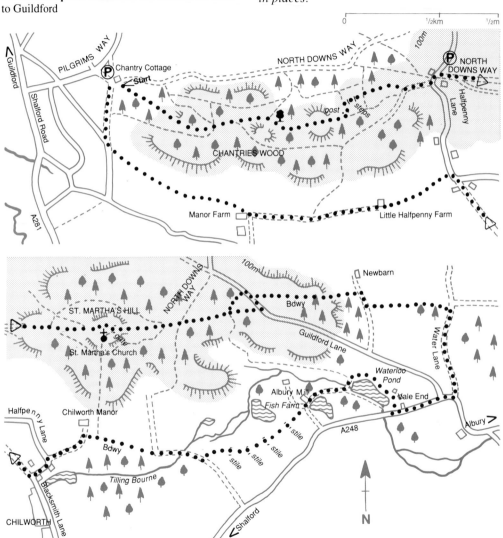

Walk 17

Drive south from the centre of Guildford on the A281 (Shalford Road) and turn up Pilgrims Way. After a short distance there is a small grassy area to the right and a car park. Walk on beyond the car park to Chantry Cottage, where there is a choice of three paths. Take the central path, climbing up the hill ahead into Chantries Wood.

There are many paths through this area of parkland and mixed woodland: stick to the main one, running approximately along the ridge of the hill. Follow this until it reaches a large oak tree with a circular bench around its bole. At this point the track splits: go to the right and continue until a further split by a red post. Go left this time, down hill. At the foot of the hill there is a further split. Turn right, up a flight of wooden steps, then continue along the track ahead, eventually joining an unmetalled track. Continue along this until it joins Halfpenny Lane, a metalled public road.

At this point there should be a house up to your left and another above and ahead of you, on the far side of the lane.

Turn left, up the road, then right (almost immediately) at the signpost for the North Downs Way. Walk up the clear track ahead, with a fence to the right and a car park opening up to the left. After passing the car park the track enters an area of woodland and splits. Stay to the left and carry on climbing up the hill ahead.

In a clear spot on the crown of the hill, commanding splendid views to the south, is St Martha's church. The site is pre-Christian, and the church is Norman in form, but it was extensively rebuilt in the 19th and early 20th centuries.

Walk through the chruchyard and exit by the eastern gate, then continue down the broad, sandy track beyond. A short distance beyond the church the track splits and the North Downs Way heads off to the left. Ignore this and carry straight on to join Guildford Lane: a metalled public road.

The paths are so numerous in this area that it is difficult to be sure exactly where you will hit the lane. When you do so, look to both left and right for the next section of the path (you should be within 20 yards of it either way): a bridleway with wooden fences to either side, heading off across the fields beyond the road. Turn down this and follow it: through the field and then along the edge of a small wood. At the end of the wood there is a T-junction. Turn right for 50 yards, then left, across another field. At the end of this path there is a further T-junction with a metalled road (Water Lane). Turn right along this, down to the A248.

Turn right along the road. After about 300 yards there is a house to the right called 'Vale End', and just beyond this there are signposts for two footpaths heading off to the right. Follow the first of these: along a gravel track, with houses to the right and Waterloo Pond to the left. Continue on this path, through the woods beyond the gardens of the houses, until it reaches a metalled road. Turn left, across a small stream and on to the trout farm at Albury Mill.

Turn left over the mill lade, then immediately right at the sign for the public footpath. Follow a rough path through an area of meadows, crossing four stiles, to join a metalled road. Turn right along this, across the Tilling Bourne and on beyond. When the road cuts up to the right leave it and carry straight on along a rough bridleway, which eventually joins a metalled driveway. Turn left down this, leaving Chilworth Manor to the right.

When the drive joins a road (Halfpenny Lane) turn left along it. When this road turns hard left into Blacksmith Lane, look for the footpath which cuts up to the right and follow it instead, to rejoin Halfpenny Lane further up the hill. Turn left along the lane, then left again at the sign for a public footpath. Follow this (partly along field boundaries and partly along a clear track), past the ruined Little Halfpenny Farm and Manor Farm beyond, and on to a public road on the edge of Guildford. Turn right up this, then first right up a footpath, to return to Chantry Cottage.

18 River Wey

Length: 3¹/₂ miles (5.5km)
Height climbed: Negligible
Grade: B
Public conveniences: Guildford
Public transport: Numerous rail and bus services

A level walk through the fields and woods along canal and river banks; also passing through the picturesque old village of Shalford. Paths generally good.

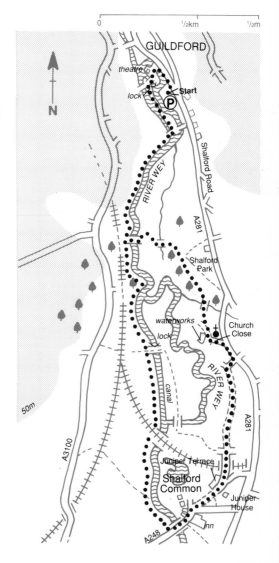

Start from the car park on Shalford Road (A281); a short distance beyond the Yvonne Arnaud Theatre when driving out from Guildford town centre.

Walk back to the theatre and turn left, down its left-hand side, then continue across the footbridge over the canal beyond. Turn left immediately after crossing this and follow the clear towpath for about a mile and a half (2.5km) – through meadowland and pleasant woodland – until a road-bridge (A248) crosses the river. Climb up onto this and turn left.

There is a row of cottages to the left to start with. These end just as the road swings to the right. Leave the road at this point and carry straight on along a rough footpath over Shalford Common. Head slightly to the left of the white gables of Juniper House and, when the houses of Juniper Terrace appear to the left, join the road which runs in front of them. At the end of the terrace the road splits. Keep to the left; crossing a redbrick railway bridge and continuing along a clear track through scrubby woodland beyond.

When the path splits turn right, up to the main street in Shalford. Turn left along this for a short distance, until Church Close cuts down to the left. Follow this down to the Thames Water building and turn right along the metalled road. When this veers to the left, carry straight on: across a grassy area at first and then along a path running through woodland up to Shalford Park.

Walk around the left-hand edge of the park until, near its far end, a clear track cuts through the dense woodland to the left. Turn onto this and follow it down to the River Wey. Turn left for a short distance along the river to reach a footbridge, then cross this and turn right, back along the original path.

19 Winkworth Arboretum

Length: 2 miles (3km)
Height climbed: 160ft (50m)
Grade: C
Public conveniences: Start of walk
Public transport: Regular bus services linking
Godalming and the arboretum

*A suggested short route along some of the
variety of paths through this pleasant area of
mixed woodland.*

Winkworth Arboretum was originally planted by
Dr Wilfrid Fox before the Second World War, and
is now maintained by the National Trust. It is a
splendid semi-wild garden laid out across the steep
slopes overlooking two small lakes and is crossed
by numerous footpaths. Some of these paths have
been used in the following route, but obviously
there are plenty of alternative walks.

To reach the arboretum, drive south from
Godalming on the B2130. The car park is to the
left of the road, about two miles (3km) from the
town centre.

Walk out of the back of the car park along the
main track, and continue along this (ignoring the
private track cutting off to the left) until it splits.
At this point head left, down a flight of steps and
on to join the main track running along the bottom
of the slope. From this point it is possible to make
a loop through the pleasant broad-leaved woodland
by the more northerly of the two lakes (Phillimore):
simply turn left and follow the main track to the
end of the lake, then turn left up a rough path before
doubling back along a track further up the slope.

Retrace your steps and then continue along the
main track, which now runs beside the southern
lake (Rowe's Flashe). Ignore tracks cutting off to
the right, and continue until the edge of the
arboretum is reached. At this point the main track
climbs up the slope to the right and then doubles
back on itself. Almost immediately a flight of steps
leads up to the left. Climb up these to a four-way
junction and then turn left, following a path whch
runs through rough, broad-leaved woodland until it
almost reaches the public road, then climbs
slightly and doubles back. This path quickly
becomes a clear track running through open
parkland, and runs along the top of the slope above
the lakes (giving fine views) before rejoining the
original track from the car park.

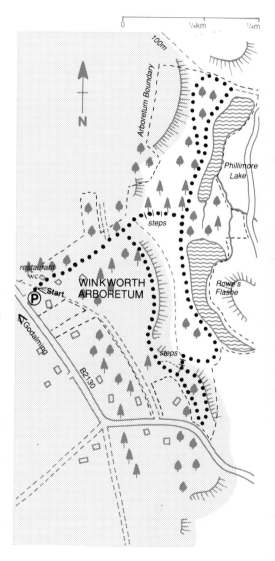

Walk 19

20 Sidney Wood

Length: 2 miles (3km)
Height climbed: Negligible
Grade: C
Public conveniences: None
Public transport: None

A clearly marked walk on good tracks and paths through conifers and an extensive area of fine, mature oakwood.

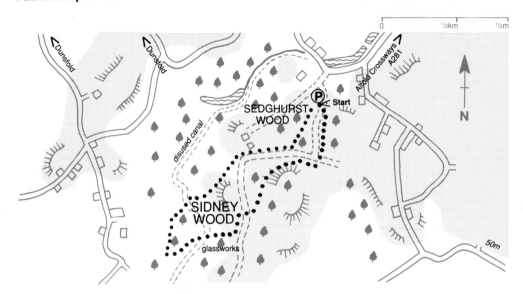

Sidney Wood is now owned by the Forestry Commission, but although there is some commercial forestry along this walk, the main glory is the old oak plantation, which includes many fine, mature trees.

To reach the wood, drive south from Guildford on the A281 road for Horsham. Follow this for around 10 miles (16km) to Alfold Crossways, then turn right onto the unnumbered road signposted for Dunsfold. Follow this for about a mile (1.5km), then take the second turning to the left and follow the signs for the car park.

There is a large-scale map of the wood in the car park, and the route itself is clearly marked along the way, with occasional notices giving information on the commercial forestry and oak woodland, and also on some of the wildlife to be found in the wood. Amongst the animals which inhabit the wood are roe deer which, though shy,

can sometimes be seen along this walk.

In addition to such natural attractions, the wood contains some interesting early industrial sites, including the dried bed of the Wey and Arun Canal (1816). At one time, this canal was part of the inland waterway link between London and Portsmouth, but it never proved popular, and after a little over half a century it was closed down (a section still containing water can be seen running parallel to the road, just before the turn into the car park).

An earlier industrial activity associated with Sidney Wood was glassmaking. There is nothing to be seen now except grassy mounds, but there were two glassworks in the wood in the mid-16th century. This was a common industry in this area at the time, and the works would have been situated in the woods to be near a handy supply of oak for fuelling the furnaces.

21 East Horsley Woodlands

Length: ³/₄ - 2 miles (1 - 3km)
Height climbed: Undulating
Grade: B/C
Public conveniences: None
Public transport: None

Three marked routes through an extensive area of dense forestry; predominantly of conifers. Paths generally good, and there are a number of architecturally interesting bridges along the routes.

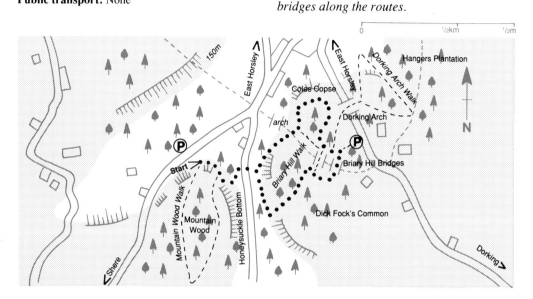

The Forestry Commission-owned Horsley Woodlands clothe the gentle slopes on the northern side of the North Downs; about six miles (9.5km) east of Guildford. The slopes were originally planted in the 19th century by Lord Lovelace of Horsley Towers (son-in-law of the poet Byron). Lovelace was the largest land owner in Surrey in his day, and a keen forester.

The original woods were felled during the Second World War (during which period the area was used for a military encampment), but the slopes were subsequently replanted, and a number of forest walks have been laid out, passing some of the remaining arched bridges which Lovelace designed and had built to enable him to pass easily through his woods. The route shown on the map is the longest of the Briary Hill Walks, with the other

footpaths also indicated.

To reach the walks, drive east from Guildford on the A25 until, just opposite the turn-off for Shere, a minor road cuts off to the left, signposted for East Horsley. Follow the East Horsley signs for about three miles (5km) until, in a narrow wooded dene, a car park appears to the left. There is a further car park one mile (1.5km) south of the A246 on the minor road between East Horsley and Dorking *(see map)*.

The routes are circular and are marked by coloured posts (Mountain Wood Walk, yellow; Briary Hill Walks, red; Dorking Arch Walk, white) and are all easily followed; running along clear paths through a mixture of conifer and broad-leaved woodland.

22 Shere

Length: 3 miles (5km)
Height climbed: 440ft (135m)
Grade: B
Public conveniences: Gomshall
Public transport: Regular bus services to Guildford and Dorking

A series of tracks, footpaths and public roads around a splendid old village; passing through pleasant farmland and climbing up to the mixed woodland along the North Downs.

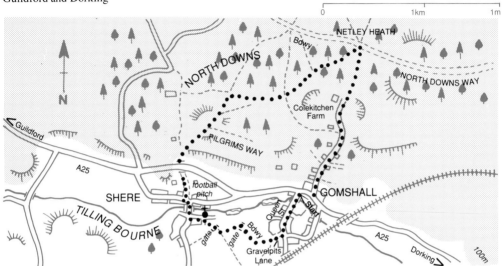

This walk starts from the village of Gomshall: six miles (9.5km) to the east of Guildford on the A25.

Walk to the west end of the village (ie, the end nearest Guildford) and turn up Queen Street. Continue along this street until a sign for a public bridleway appears to the right, pointing up Gravelpits Lane. Turn into this. Quickly veer left (just before reaching some cottages), then right, along a clear track. Follow this track through fields until it passes through a gate. Shortly beyond this a path heads off to the right; turn on to this and follow it down towards the spire of Shere Church.

Turn left along the road before the church, then right at the village square. When the road reaches a T-junction turn left, then first right, up a clear track running to the left of a football ground. This track runs under the A25, then climbs up the slope of the North Downs beyond. When the track splits

(shortly after the road) keep to the right, then carry on climbing. Ignore the track of the Pilgrims' Way (which heads off to the right) and continue, through woodland, until a four-way junction is reached on the brow of the hill.

Turn right and walk on along a clear track through fine mature woodland. The track crosses two junctions and is then joined from the left by a bridleway. Continue beyond this, always sticking to the main track and ignoring the paths to right and left, until a five-way junction is reached by a seat.

Turn right at this point, back down the face of the hill. The path runs through woodland at first, then emerges into farmland and becomes metalled just before passing Colekitchen Farm. Continue along this road, back down to the village of Gomshall.

Walk 22

23 Pitch Hill

Length: 3½ miles (5.5km)
Height climbed: 330ft (100m)
Grade: B
Public conveniences: None
Public transport: Regular bus services from
Guildford and Cranleigh

A circuit along some of the clear and pleasant footpaths through this area of dense mixed woodland, leading to a hilltop and fine views.

Drive to Gomshall – about six miles (9.5km) to the east of Guildford on the A25 – and turn south on the minor road to Peaslake. At the junction in the centre of the village, turn right along Walking Bottom. After a short distance there is a car park to the left of the road.

Walk to the far end of the car park, then continue along the clear track through the woodland beyond. Shortly after the start the track splits: keep left, and when a track joins from the left, carry on along that. Continue (ignoring the many tracks cutting off to right and left) for about a mile (1.5km), until the track passes some houses to the right.

Just beyond the houses, a Right of Way (signposted) cuts off to the right. Turn up this rough path, and continue along it until it joins a clearer track, then turn left. Climb up to an open area with a bench and a fine southerly view. Shortly beyond this there is a four-way junction. Turn left, along the face of the hill, and follow the path up to the summit of Pitch Hill, where a view opens up of the wooded hills to the west.

Three other paths leave the summit of the hill. Take the middle one and follow it along the top edge of a steep wooded slope. After a short distance this path leads down past an old quarry to a car park.

Walk through the car park and straight on out the other side; across a grassy area at first, then on along a clear track through fine, mature, mixed woodland. After a short way the track splits. Keep to the left, then carry on (across two four-way junctions) for a little over a mile (1.5km), back to the start point.

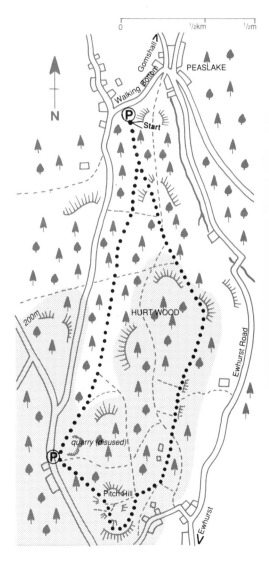

Walk 23

24 Holmbury Hill

Length: 3 miles (5km)
Height climbed: 350ft (100m)
Grade: B
Public conveniences: None
Public transport: Regular bus service to
Holmbury St. Mary from Guildford and Dorking

*A route following some of the many tracks
and footpaths through this attractive area of
dense mixed woodland, and providing fine
views from an open hilltop. Some navigation
necessary.*

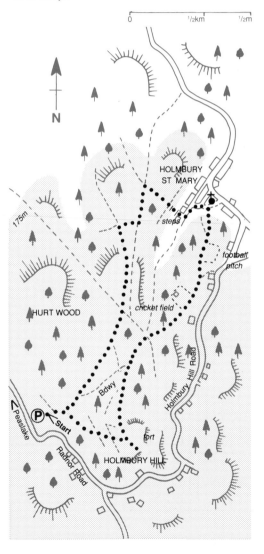

To reach the start of this walk, drive six miles
(9.5km) east of Guildford on the A25, to the little
village of Gomshall, then turn right onto the minor
road signposted for Peaslake. Once Peaslake is
reached, turn left (just before the telephone box)
onto Radnor Road. Follow this for a little over a
mile (1.5km) until a large car park appears, up to
the left of the road.

A clear track leaves the car park and leads – in
less than half a mile (1km) – to the open peak of
Holmbury Hill (the site of an Iron Age fort).
There are fine views from this point across the
surrounding hills and farmland.

Leave the hilltop by the same track, but then
take the first clear track which leads off to the
right. When the track splits, keep to the right; then
continue, through dense woodland, until a T-
junction is reached, with a bridleway crossing the
track. Turn right and continue for a short distance
until you reach a five-way junction, then take the
second track from the right: a footpath leading
through mixed woodland down to a cricket field.

Pass this to the right and continue down the
hill beyond. When the track splits keep to the left;
passing through woods to a football pitch, then
down the rough footpath beyond to reach the
village of Holmbury St Mary just behind the
church.

Turn left along a clear track, down to the
public road. Turn left along this for a short
distance, then right, up a clear track between two
houses. Climb up the steps behind the houses then
continue, across a faint track and on to join a
stronger one. Turn left along this, then first right.
When this path joins another track, turn left and
follow it back to the car park. There are a great
many paths running through the woods in this area,
but stick to the main track and there should be no
problems *(see map)*.

25 Leith Hill

Length: 6 miles (9.5km)
Height climbed: 450ft (140m)
Grade: A
Public conveniences: None
Public transport: Postbus service between Dorking and Coldharbour

A walk through the dense mixed woodland and farmland around this fine viewpoint with its splendid old folly. Paths good, but some navigation required and a detailed area map is recommended.

From the village of Wotton – three miles (5km) west of Dorking on the A25 – drive south for three miles (5km) on the road signposted for Leith Hill. Park in the large car park at Starveall Corner.

At the back of the car park there is a sign for the Tower. Follow the footpath beyond for a little under a mile (1.5km), through fine mixed woodland, to the 18th-century folly on the summit of the hill. This is the highest point in South East England and the view is splendid.

Carry straight on past the tower; down a steep slope, across a track at the bottom, then up the slope beyond and on along the main track to Coldharbour, passing the cricket ground on the way. From the village, turn left up the track signposted as a footpath to Buryhill Woods and carry straight on along it for about two miles (3km): through woods at first, then passing Upper Merriden Farm between two fields, then back into woods again. Near the end of this section, a field appears to the right. Look for a trig point to the right of the track and continue. After a short way the woods end to the left and there is a small field, then another band of trees beyond that. Turn left beyond these trees along a rough path to join a clearer track. Turn left along this, with the trees up to the left.

When the track joins a public road, turn left; through the little hamlet of Broadmoor and then on along the clear track beyond. After a short way this track joins a clearer track which comes in from the left. Continue along this until it reaches a hairpin bend, then carry straight on along a rough footpath.

Turn right at a clear four-way junction. Continue until the path almost reaches the road, then turn left and follow a clear path; through the woods, over another junction, and back to the car park.

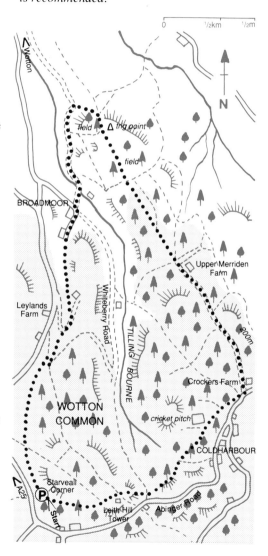

26 Polesden Lacey

Length: 5 miles (8km)
Height climbed: 350ft (100m) undulating
Grade: A
Public conveniences: None
Public transport: Occasional bus services to
Ranmore Common from Dorking

*A clear route on footpaths, tracks and public
roads; running through dense mixed woodland and farmland and passing the fine old
house of Polesden Lacey (1824): now owned
by the National Trust and open to the public.*

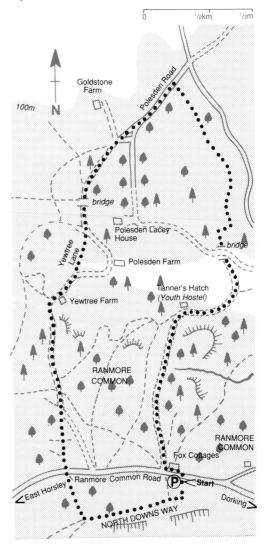

To reach the start of this walk, drive two miles
(3km) from the centre of Dorking on the minor
road to East Horsley (Ranmore Common Road)
and watch for the large car park to the left of the
road.

Cross the road and turn left for a short distance,
then turn right just beyond two cottages. At this
point there is a choice of three tracks: take the
middle one, signposted for the YHA, and follow it
through mature woodland for a little under a mile
(1.5km) until a T-junction is reached. Turn right,
past the hostel at Tanner's Hatch, and follow the
clear track as it swings left: away from the wood
and across a shallow valley of fields, then up the
far side and back into woodland.

The track is quite clear at this point: passing
under a bridge and then continuing, climbing
slowly with fields to the right, until it joins the
metalled Polesden Road. Turn left down this, and
continue along it until it forks.

The road to the left leads into Polesden Lacey
House *(see p.viii)* but, for this walk, take the track
signposted for Goldstone Farm. When the farm
track heads off to the right carry straight on down a
rough track between hedges; under a thatched
bridge and on through a narrow cutting. Shortly
after the bridge the track swings round to the left.
Leave it at this point and continue straight ahead
down a yew-lined path, which eventually rejoins
the original track and swings to the right of
Yewtree Farm.

Ignore two tracks heading off to the right *(see
map)* and continue until the main track starts to
swing to the left. At this point another track
carries straight on: follow this through the trees
(ignoring paths to right and left) to the road.

On the far side of the road the track coninues.
Follow this until it is crossed by the clear route of
the North Downs Way. Turn left here to return to
the start.

27 Box Hill

Length: 1) 1 mile (1.5km); **2)** 2¹/₂ miles (4km)
Height climbed: 1) 230ft (70m); **2)** 300ft (90m)
Grade: 1) C; **2)** B
Public conveniences: Start of Walk
Public transport: Regular bus services from
Dorking and Leatherhead

Two clearly marked routes through the woodland and grassland around one of the finest viewpoints in the area. There is an information centre at the start of the routes, and a detailed booklet is available.

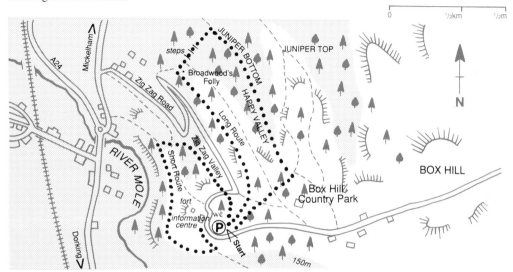

Box Hill is perhaps the best-known peak in the chain of the North Downs, with its steep southern slope rising up above the town of Dorking and the valley of the River Mole (which here cuts northwards through the line of hills), and its fine expanse of woodland, criss-crossed with white, chalky paths. The hill is now owned by the National Trust, who have laid out two fine walks through the woods to the north of the hill.

To reach the hill, drive north from Dorking on the A24. A little over a mile (1.5km) from the town centre there is a roundabout. Turn right onto the road for Mickleham. After a short distance turn right again, onto a minor road signposted for Box Hill.

The two routes start from the large car park near the summit (there is a small charge for parking). The shorter of the two (marked by red posts) starts by dropping down to the main

southerly viewpoint, with its excellent views across Dorking to the Lower Greensand Hills *(Walks 23,24,25)*, then swings northwards down a narrow, open, chalk ridge. It eventually drops down from this, to the right, then returns to the start up the wooded dene of Zig Zag Valley, with its fine old yew trees.

The longer route (marked by purple posts) heads northwards through fine mixed woodland (with views to the west across Zig Zag Valley) to Broadwood's Folly: a 19th-century round flint tower, overlooking Juniper Hall at the foot of the hill opposite *(see p. ix)*. From the folly, the route drops down a flight of steps to the right to join a clear track which runs up the floor of a narrow valley called Juniper Bottom. Turn right up this, and follow the clear signposted tracks back to the car park.

Walk 27

28 Headley Heath

Length: Up to 3 miles (5km)
Height climbed: Undulating
Grade: B/C
Public conveniences: None
Public transport: Regular bus service from
Leatherhead

*A route using some of the numerous paths
through this fine diverse area of mixed
habitats. Paths generally good.*

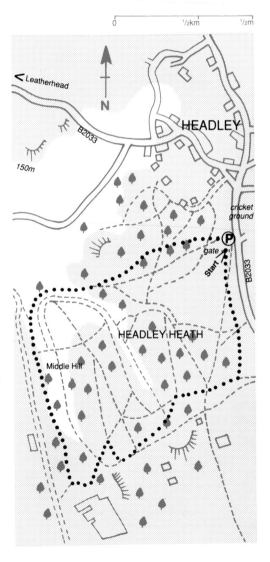

Headley Heath (now owned by the National Trust)
is an area of common land: a mixture of lowland
heath, chalk grassland and woodland caused by the
complex geology of this area. There are a great
number of permissive footpaths and bridleways
across the area, some of which are shown on the
map. A suggested route is also shown, around the
outer edge of the area, but there are many
alternatives, and there is general access along the
paths.

To reach the heath, drive three miles (5km)
east of Dorking on the A25, then turn left onto the
B2032. After about a mile and a half (2.5km) the
B2033 cuts off to the left. Follow this for about a
mile (1.5km) until a large car park appears to the
left of the road. There is a small charge for
parking.

For the route shown, walk south from the car
park (ie, turn right if you are facing the road) on a
clear track through scrub woodland. When the
track splits go left, then continue (ignoring
numerous paths to the right and left) until a T-
junction is reached. Turn right and follow a clear
track, through more mature woodland, along the
southern edge of the heath.

There are numerous junctions along this track
(with tracks cutting to the right, into the heart of the
heath), but for the route shown, keep to the left and
continue to the far corner of the heath, then turn
right along a path with a metalled road running
parallel to the left. This path eventually starts
dropping down into the wooded valley to the right.
Ignore the track which cuts off to the left, half way
down the slope, and continue to the bottom. Curve
round the end of the grassy chalk ridge which
comes in from the right and then (ignoring the
tracks to right and left) climb up the steep slope
ahead. At the top of the slope there are numerous
paths: just carry on in approximately the same
direction to return to the car park.

Walk 28

29 Walton Heath

Length: 4 miles (6.5km)
Height climbed: Negligible
Grade: B
Public conveniences: Walton on the Hill
Public transport: Regular bus service from
Kingston-Upon-Thames

*A sequence of footpaths and public roads
through mixed woodland and open grassland,
passing by the side of a golf course. Paths
good, but some navigation required.*

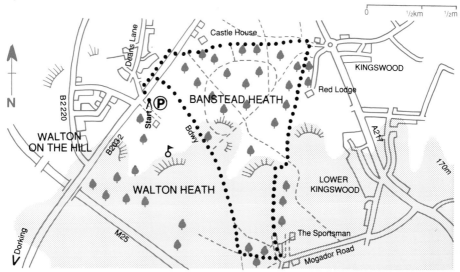

The small town of Walton on the Hill sits on the
southern edge of Greater London. To reach it,
drive three miles (5km) east of Dorking on the
A25, then turn left on the B2032 for a little over
two miles (3km). Ignore the turn onto the B2220
and continue for a short distance until a car park
appears to the right.

Cross the road to join the pavement and turn
right. Continue until a sign indicates a public
bridleway heading off through the trees to the right
of the road, by the side of a golf course. Follow
this clear track to the end of the wood, then
continue across an area of open grassland and on
along a line of scrub woodland beyond.

Continue until the path reaches a four-way
junction with a clear track, then turn left and
follow this track through woodland (ignoring paths
to left and right) to a junction with a public road.
Turn left, passing the Sportsman Inn. When the

road ends carry on, with the open common to the
left and a line of trees to the right.

Continue until a clear track cuts right, through
the wood and onto the open ground beyond.
Follow the track across the open area, then
continue, with a thin band of woodland to the
right. Carry on until a junction is reached, then go
straight ahead, with a fence to the right and a
cottage (Red Lodge) beyond it. Follow this clear
path to a further T-junction, then turn left.

Almost immediately there is a choice of three
paths. Take the path furthest to the left. After
about 100yds a track cuts off to the left: ignore this
and continue to the next junction. Turn right here;
uphill across a grassy area with trees to the left,
heading towards some pines on the horizon.
Continue by the trees when a hedge starts to the
right with a house beyond it, then at the next
junction bear right to return to the road.

Walk 29

30 Limpsfield Chart

Length: 3 miles (5km)
Height climbed: Undulating
Grade: B
Public conveniences: None
Public transport: Regular bus service from Oxted to Limpsfield Chart

A route using some of the numerous footpaths and bridleways through this area of dense, mixed woodland. Some navigation required; paths generally good. Excellent views.

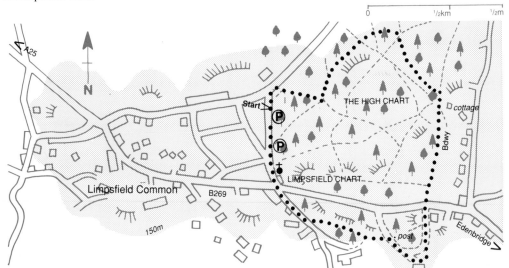

Limpsfield Chart is a small village on the edge of an area of mixed conifer and broad-leaved woodland, on the eastern edge of Surrey. To reach it, follow the A25 east from Reigate. Just beyond Oxted the B269 road for Edenbridge cuts off to the right. Follow this for a little over a mile (1.5km), then turn left by the prominent church.

Park in the second car park to the right of this minor road, then walk on until, just as another road comes in from the left, a clear track cuts in to the wood to the right. Follow this up to a four-way junction and turn left, then at the next junction turn left again. Ignore paths cutting off to either side and follow this clear track, through mixed woodland, as it slowly bends round to the right.

Continue until a five-way junction is reached, near the corner of a field. Take the second path

from the right: a faint, grassy footpath, which eventually joins a broad, straight bridleway near a cottage. Follow this track to the right, climbing gently uphill through mature conifers, to the public road (B269), then walk straight across and on along the signposted footpath opposite.

Ignore the first track cutting off to the right and, at the next junction, carry straight on: downhill on a narrow path towards a house. Turn right along a good track (noting the fine views to the south) and continue until a yellow arrow marks the start of a path to the left. Turn on to this and follow it (ignoring turns to either side) until it reaches a metalled road providing access to houses.

Turn right and follow this road down to the B269. Cross the road and walk on along the minor road opposite to return to the car park.

Country Code

All walkers, when leaving public roads to pass through farmland, forestry or moorland, should respect the interests of those whose livelihoods depend on the land. Carelessness can easily cause damage. You are therefore urged to follow the Country Code:

Guard against all risk of fire

Keep all dogs under proper control

Fasten all gates

Keep to the paths across farmland

Avoid damaging fences, hedges and walls

Leave no litter

Safeguard water supplies

Protect wildlife, wild plants and trees

Go carefully on country roads

Respect the life of the countryside

BARTHOLOMEW WALKS SERIES

WALK CORK & KERRY
0 7028 0949 7

WALK THE CORNISH COASTAL PATH
A special format step-by-step guide to the entire length of the Cornish Coastal Path (Marsland Mouth – Cremyll)
0 7028 0902 0

WALK THE COTSWOLDS
0 7028 0908 X

WALK THE DALES
0 7028 0800 8

MORE WALKS IN THE DALES
0 7028 0948 9

YORKSHIRE DALES VISITOR'S PACK
Containing a copy of *Walk the Dales* and a folded 1 inch map of the Yorkshire Dales in a clear, plastic carrying wallet.
0 7028 0932 2

WALK DEVON & CORNWALL
0 7028 1283 8

WALK DORSET & HARDY'S WESSEX
0 7028 0906 3

WALK EDINBURGH & THE PENTLANDS
0 7028 1280 3

WALK EXMOOR & THE QUANTOCKS
0 7028 0910 1

WALK HERTS & BUCKS
0 7028 0953 5

WALK THE ISLE OF WIGHT
0 7028 1279 X

WALK THE LAKES
0 7028 8111 2

MORE WALKS IN THE LAKES
0 7028 0819 9

LAKE DISTRICT WALKING PACK
Containing a copy of *Walk the Lakes* and a folded 1 inch map of the Lake District in a clear, plastic carrying wallet.
0 7028 0876 8

WALK LOCH LOMOND & THE TROSSACHS
0 7028 0744 3

WALK LOCH NESS & THE RIVER SPEY
0 7028 0787 7

WALK LOTHIAN, THE BORDERS & FIFE
0 7028 0803 2

WALK THE NEW FOREST
0 7028 0810 5

WALK THE NORTH DOWNS
0 7028 0742 7

WALK THE NORTH YORK MOORS
0 7028 0743 5

WALK NORTHUMBRIA
0 7028 0959 4

NORTHUMBRIA WALKING PACK
Containing a copy of *Walk Northumbria* and a folded copy of the Northumberland & Durham Leisure Map in a clear, plastic carrying wallet.
0 7028 1216 1

WALK OBAN, MULL & LOCHABER
0 7028 0801 6

WALK THE PEAK DISTRICT
0 7028 0710 9

MORE WALKS IN THE PEAK DISTRICT
0 7028 0951 9

WALK PERTHSHIRE
0 7028 0766 4

**WALK ROYAL DEESIDE
& NORTH EAST SCOTLAND**
0 7028 0898 9

WALK SNOWDONIA & NORTH WALES
0 7028 0804 0

**WALK SOUTH DEVON
COASTAL PATH & DARTMOOR**
0 7028 1811 9

WALK THE SOUTH DOWNS
0 7028 0811 3

WALK THE SOUTH PENNINES
0 7028 0955 1

**WALK SOUTH WALES
& THE WYE VALLEY**
0 7028 0904 7

WALK SOUTH WEST SCOTLAND
0 7028 0900 4

WALK SURREY
0 7028 1807 0

**WALK THE WATERWAYS
AROUND MANCHESTER**
0 7028 1809 7